MARKETING BUZZWORD TO MARKETING AUTHORITY

BEN M ROBERTS

I want to dedicate this book to all the people that have helped me in my career to-date. Without their help and guidance I would not have been able to make this book a reality.

In particular, I want to dedicate it to my parents Chris & Sarah, and my girlfriend Meg.

CONTENTS

FOR THOSE WHO MADE THIS BOOK POSSIBLE

Were it not for the faith and money pledged in the crowd-funding campaign for this book, you would not be reading this today.

I would like to wholeheartedly say a massive thank you to the following people who made this dream of mine, a fully fledged reality.

Alex McCann
Andrew Pickering
Ben Hofmeister
Ben Ellis
Bruce Bollington
Chris Huskins
Chris Roberts
Damian Burgess
Dan Gingiss
Daniel Lemin
Dennis Owen
Desiree Martinez
Felix Winstone

Jen Cole
Jenny Potts
Jessica Roberts
Jessica Cory
John Espirian
Juan Felix
Kat Agg
Kelly Tamplin
Kylene Kaelin
Molly Rumbelow
Moses Velasco
Nicky Kriel
Paolo Fabrizio
Paul Ince
Paul Richards
Paul Lanzerstorfer
Philip Whitfield
Robert Young
Sam Williamson
Sarah Roberts
Shep Hyken
Sue Squire
Timothy Lewis

Your kind contributions have helped turn this crazy idea into a reality. Your pledged funds helped contribute to the copy-editing, proof-reading and artwork. Without these funds the quality of all the all three would have been significantly lessened.

I am indebted to you all. Thank you.

FOREWORD

BY CHRIS STRUB, CEO OF I AM HERE, LLC

'What does success look like to you?'

In my travels to speak on stages worldwide, it's the singular, leading question that I rely upon to challenge the audience's existing thought processes.

I've met marketers around the globe from all walks of life – from solopreneurs and start-up founders, to agency stalwarts and top-level digital executives – and one peculiar theme often prevails:

A curiously antagonistic approach to certain buzzwords.

Less experienced marketers commonly exude enthusiasm, but may lack a broader understanding of the industry vernacular. Meanwhile, more seasoned veterans may tire of trying to keep up with the latest millennial mumbo-jumbo.

Blithe indifference to the latest industry buzzwords is the easy way out – opening the opportunity for your competition to buzz right by you.

This book, however, will open your eyes to the broader buzzword culture; show you how to masterfully manipulate your own messaging; and forever change the way you liaise with your lingo.

Whether you're just beginning your personal branding journey, leading a team of seasoned marketing professionals, or somewhere in between, 'Marketing Buzzword to Marketing Authority' is a definitive guide to help you identify your own path forward.

If you've ever felt intimidated by the endlessly complex jungle of jargon within the digital marketing space, this is the book for you.

Right from its opening pages, 'Marketing Buzzword to Marketing Authority' brings you along on Ben Roberts' courageous journey to conquer that confusion, one industry buzzword – and one buzz-worthy podcast interview – at a time.

The ensuing chapters brilliantly juxtapose the underlying science and psychology of buzzword culture, with an intercultural mosaic of global thought-leaders who have mastered the art of wielding their own buzzwords for personal and professional growth.

You'll be treated to a personalised introduction to some of the most substantive digital visionaries in the industry, and hear exactly how they've conquered their own corner of the buzzword biosphere. While Ben has circumnavigated the globe to identify and converse with these pros – you can save yourself the plane ticket, and build your network by turning the page. (Stale pretzels and ginger ale optional.)

Whether you've listened to every episode of 'The Marketing Buzzword Podcast' ("Helllooooo, you beautiful marketing bees!"), or are learning of Ben's work for the first time in this introduction, you'll develop an understanding of the marketing industry's expansive set of buzzword-centric subcultures – and the common threads between them.

By the end of this book, you'll yield the knowledge and the motivation to bust through that jargon jungle, and expertly leverage your own buzzwords to establish your own well-defined path to success.

Chris Strub

CEO, I Am Here, LLC

Twitter: @ChrisStrub

INTRODUCTION

Buzzwords. A definite love-hate topic, and one that sparks plenty of emotions and feelings.

When I first started working in marketing, I remember reading article after article about the latest marketing advice, practices and techniques. I came across so many words and phrases that I had never heard before; even whilst studying my marketing university degree. It was as if I was entering a whole new world – a world of buzzwords. In all honesty, it was mind-blowing. There was just so much I needed to process.

In response to this, I wrote down all my thoughts, ideas and research into a notebook. I still have this book, and, when I look back at it, I can see the words and terms we were using 8/9 years before. Many have come and gone, and a number have become part of everyday business and marketing vocabulary. Why has this happened? What caused some to disappear, whilst others still thrive? What will the next buzzword be that will stand the test of time?

When I was writing in my notebook back in the year 2000

I didn't actually give buzzwords much thought. It wasn't until the summer of 2017, when I was at a marketing conference, that my interest in buzzwords really took hold. As I sat there and listened to every speaker, I began to write down as many buzzwords as possible. I wrote down 42.

BINGO!

That's a lot of buzzwords, and with the number that I heard over, and over, I would definitely have been able to have a great game of buzzword bingo.

That was when my interest was piqued. I began to research and read about buzzwords, and I became hooked. I couldn't stop writing down buzzwords. I wanted to define them and break them down to the sum of their parts to help not only myself, but also others, to understand whether or not they are actually useful.

To my surprise, I couldn't find any books, articles or proper research that focused on breaking down and truly understanding what buzzwords meant, and why we used them.

That was the primary reason why The Marketing Buzzword podcast was born. To quote Brian Fanzo: 'I pushed the damn button'. In hindsight, perhaps I should have planned it a bit better, but I just put myself out there, with no agenda other than helping people to understand buzzwords.

It was crazy; the feedback I received was incredible, and something I hadn't foreseen at all. The podcast seemed to resonate with people (had I planned things properly, maybe this wouldn't have been such a shock to me). I was in the right place at the right time, and I did something about it. When I asked people to contribute, they did so without hesitation. The advice and opinions I received was amazing, and it spurred me on to want to create more and more posts, and make the podcast better and better.

As the podcast took off and started growing at a rate that was completely beyond my wildest dreams, I began to think again... Why are people using buzzwords? What are they looking to get from using them? How can I help people to not only understand them, but to use them in a valuable way?

This book was born from that idea.

It's been much harder to write this book than it was to get my podcast going, but I wanted to do it. I wanted this book to inspire, motivate and help people to embrace buzzwords for good – not cast aspersions on them. I want to make sure that you maximise the potential benefits they can bring not just for you, but for your business.

Buzzwords are everywhere. You can't ignore them, or pretend you've never used one before, because I guarantee that you will have.

That's why this book is important, and why I decided to write it. To ignore buzzwords, or to not use words and phrases that are in common use, means limiting and restricting yourself and your business. Why would you restrict yourself, if you don't have to?

You need to read this book because not all buzzwords are created equally: some are pure jargon, while others are an immense opportunity. These opportunities can help you create a personal brand or a business, and they can help keep you focused and grow an audience.

Throughout the entirety of this book you will find people and brands who have leveraged the power of buzzwords, not as jargon, but to build a following. They have built successful, personal brands and businesses off the back of becoming synonymous with a common word or phrase. This association, whether created by design, skill or by coincidence, has become the backbone on which they have built an audience, and they are now reaping the benefits.

This book will give you new ideas and inspiration. It will help you to carve out your own niche, by coining a buzzword yourself, or it will help you to find your own little space by leveraging the power and opportunities of an already existing buzzword. This is so you and/or your business can be seen as an authority. A real authority. Not someone who has bought thousands of Instagram followers, but someone who is seen as an industry pioneer or an expert on a buzzword.

Using a buzzword can give you some short-term wins. After all, they are popular terms. However, that isn't the focus of this book. This book isn't about creating one blog post or doing a week-long campaign. It is about the medium term and the long term. It's about building and maintaining an audience through consistency, quality and value. Not for narcissistic self-gratification, but for your audience, to empower them, and to help them achieve more.

If you do it for yourself, you will get some short-term benefits, but that shouldn't be your goal. Your goal should be bigger, more powerful, more impactful.

This book will first help to change your own understanding of buzzwords, and, second, will convince you that you can, and should, actually build successes from and with them.

But this book isn't a step-by-step guide. It isn't a 'do this, this and this, and you are guaranteed success' book. This is because I don't believe there is a one-size-fits-all approach to using buzzwords. I also want every person who reads this book to take their own ideas away from it and create their business and brand in a way that suits them, so that each will have a unique personality.

However, what this book will do is give you the ideas, the confidence and the understanding to enhance your existing personal brand and/or business or create one.

What are we waiting for? Let's get on with it!

PART ONE
THE WHAT AND WHY OF BUZZWORDS

Love them, hate them, like them or loathe them; you cannot escape them. They are everywhere, and you cannot hide from them. They cross cultures, borders, industries and languages and you'll use them in one form or another almost daily.

They are buzzwords. Those beastly words and phrases that either make you feel like you're one of the smartest people around, or someone who is completely out of the loop.

The world of buzzwords and how they are used is a fascinating one, and one that I have taken a real interest in. So much so, that I have written this book about them. Not just what they are, and how they work, but also the practical applications and use cases for them.

The bit about buzzwords which fascinates me most is the differences between how they are used and how they are perceived. In this section we are going to explore that, by looking at the what, and the why. I felt that this was extremely important to do before we go into how to practically apply them into your personal brand or incorporate them into your business brand.

By the end of part one, you are going to have a clear idea of what a buzzword actually is and why both people and businesses use them. This section will also cover some of the psychological reasoning and rationale for their use, and look at some of the regional and cultural differences, some misconceptions, and their evolution. This will then be rounded off with a look at the future of buzzwords, because they do not stay the same, and they will not be going away.

Jargon and buzzwords are almost a necessary part of corporate life. The key for me though is not using that jargon with your customers if they don't have prior knowledge or awareness of it. It will confuse them, or worse annoy them.

- Roger Edwards, Roger Edwards Marketing

The Marketing Buzzword Podcast

ONE

WHAT EXACTLY IS A BUZZWORD, AND IS IT THE SAME AS JARGON?

"Dump the technospeak. Nobody understands it."

— Joyce Bustinduy, Levi Strauss & Company

According to the dictionary (a good place to start), a buzzword is 'often an item of jargon that's fashionable at a particular time, or in a particular context'. Other sources claim that buzzwords are 'jargon which has little meaning but becomes popular'.

I don't necessarily subscribe to that way of thinking, at least in a marketing context. I define a marketing buzzword as 'a newly created term or phrase that seeks to define a marketing activity or change in the industry'.

This is where things get interesting. For some, buzzwords are used as access-blocking jargon and because they are fashionable. Others are used to help bring together relevant content in a way that people can understand.

What this book is not about is encouraging jargon-filled paragraphs and phrases, which don't make any sense like this:

"There is no **turnkey solution**. We need to **touch base** regularly to **get on the same page** and continuously **vector towards success** on this **value add** initiative. **People adoption** strategies will be vital to make this **mind-set shift**. It's going to feel a lot like **herding cats** or even like **getting Jell-O to stick to the wall**, but if we take it one buzzword at a time and don't try to **boil the ocean**, it might work."[1]

I am not an advocate (nor will I ever be) for examples like that. It doesn't make sense. It's nonsensical, adds no meaning and offers no value. This is jargon. These are not the buzzwords you want to be building your business or personal brand around.

Using jargon in this way is laziness, and very much a case of using them to make you or your business sound more knowledgeable than you are. However, you can and should be breaking down buzzwords, and contextualising them in order to help your audience to digest and understand their meaning so that they can apply them to their work. That's where the beauty of buzzwords lies: in their ability to bring together relevant content, under a single umbrella, to a specific audience. Like the terms 'conversational commerce', 'brand storytelling' or 'relationship marketing'. These make sense, and band together content, not like the terms 'boil-the-ocean', 'shift the paradigm' or 'run it up the flagpole'.

At the start of 2018 (January 12th), Mark Zuckerberg and Facebook made an announcement about changes being made to the Facebook algorithm[2], regarding how and when content will be shown, and to who.

This change would affect so many areas of marketing, and it could become really easy to lose track of all the areas affected by the announcement. Cue a marketing buzzword: 'Facebook Apocalypse'.

Before January 12th, this term didn't have any reason to exist. However, due to a change in context and the need to group relevant content together, it came into existence. By using this term, everyday marketers are now able to understand that the content they are reading refers to this specific context, and moment in time.

A mistake that people often make when they are building their opinion on buzzwords, is thinking that they have to be relevant and appeal to all people. A buzzword doesn't have to appeal to both businesses and end customers. It doesn't even have to be relevant across business types. Some parts of society, or even areas of your business, don't need to know. Their knowing has no impact on you, your business or your department.

Let's take the term 'content marketing' or just simply 'content' for example. Marketers and businesses use the terms a lot, but customers don't. When people watch videos or read blogs, they would rarely refer to it as 'great content', they'd say it was a really funny video or an interesting read.

From a business perspective this is content, but your customers don't have to view it as so, and it shouldn't matter if they want to refer to it as something different. The categorisation of content is specific to businesses: they want and need that, customers don't. It's all about context, and relevance.

As mentioned earlier in this chapter, effective buzzwords are the ones that bring together relevant material under a single word or term, so that it becomes relevant and contextual for a specific audience.

The difficulty comes in ensuring that the use and abundance of buzzwords in an industry doesn't become a barrier to entry for job seekers looking to enter the profession, but also helps identify those who already have a prior knowledge of the market.

Buzzwords become a barrier to entry when they are used as part of a superiority complex or as part of a 'them and us' mindset. This is the biggest issue. The term itself isn't at fault, it's the way in which we use them that causes issues. This is the mindset of, "I know what it means, why don't you?" "I know what this means, and you don't, therefore I'm more knowledgeable than you." Whether we want to admit it or not, we are all somewhat guilty of this, at one stage or another.

Ultimately, nearly every buzzword, at its core, is jargon. Or at least, that's how they start out their life. Their existence likely started out to simplify an existing, complex system. This simplification can make things easier to categorise, write and even say. An example would be saying 'The Cloud' instead of saying 'virtually hosted data storage and utility computing model'. It's the same thing, but the first is a damn-sight easier to say.

Content Marketing is another prime example of this. There are so many elements that go into it. However, when you, as a marketer, say to someone that you've created content, they know that you will have created a written, audio or visual resource that people can consume.

This difference between jargon and buzzwords is wholly fascinating. Not least because of the different views of what are essentially the same thing. The average Joe would probably describe jargon as technical industry-specific words and terms used to showcase complexity. Whereas, with buzzwords, the overarching consensus seems to be that they are used make people sound and look clever, and that there isn't any substance beneath.

There is some element of truth to both terms, but you can't tarnish everyone with the same stereotype. And, as I will clearly set out in the rest of this book, you can create amazing, valuable content around a buzzword, and build authority off the back of it.

Buzzwords don't have the best reputation. That's why I wanted to write this book. To flip perceptions. To move the conversation from 'Oh, you're talking about buzzwords. Buzzwords are what's wrong with the industry. They're what's wrong with marketing.' to 'how does that buzzword impact me and my business? How can I use it for good?'

Still with me? Good. This is just the entrance to the Aladdin's cave of buzzwords and becoming a marketing authority.

customer service; and Nicky Kriel (https://www. nickykriel.com), who specialises in social media and social selling. Seriously, if you haven't heard of any of these guys before, get on the internet NOW, check them out, then come back to this book.

All of the above people, I have had the pleasure of meeting (in person and virtually), and exploring their thoughts, ideas and experiences.

Relationship marketing is a culture thing. You need to empower your employees to make relationships happen.

- Jessika Phillips, NOW Marketing Group

The Marketing Buzzword Podcast

THREE

WHY DO BUZZWORDS GET A BAD REPUTATION?

"Try not to be either intimidated by or a captive of jargon. Even though it's language, and language is about communication, it often exists actually to obfuscate and to control power and not to communicate."
- Christie Hefner

It's important to remember that the way in which buzzwords are used in various industries differs greatly. In some areas like education, politics and business, buzzwords are part and parcel of the industry. Every industry has its own quirks and intricacies.

Take politics for example. The way that buzzwords are used by politicians can be in a completely different world to how they are used elsewhere. In politics there is a tendency to use buzzwords as a barrier to entry, and to create a superiority complex. I'm not saying that this this is in indicative of all politicians, but take a look at the news, or video clips of speeches.

In the case of politics, buzzwords can be used to baffle and bamboozle people into not asking further questions or understanding what they actually mean. When politicians do this, do they inspire trust in them? Do you feel that they are actually knowledgeable on the subject? Do they help you, the electorate to feel more aware of what's going on, and how their decisions will affect your everyday life? I'd quite happily argue that in 80-90% of cases the answer will be no.

This is why buzzwords don't always have the best reputation, and those of us that use them can be negatively stereotyped. Thankfully though, in business marketing, there is less of an 'us and them' attitude and less of a 'build barriers not bridges' approach, which is apparent in politics.

Ultimately, marketing buzzwords are not the same as political buzzwords, educational buzzwords or any other industry specific buzzwords. You cannot tarnish any, or all with the same brush, because in some industries there is very much a time and place for niche buzzwords. It's about finding the balance between making things easier for the average person to understand vs ensuring that the industry maintains certain knowledge standards.

It is important to consider context when making judgement calls about whether or not a buzzword is 'bad for business' or an industry. Balance is never easy, and it requires mass market buy-in. However, a small number of people can make a big difference (especially if they are true influencers).

Another reason why buzzwords can get a bad reputation is because 'they don't mean anything in particular'. Yes, you know the ones, the terms which are all fluff and no substance, or are just large umbrella terms which house lots of other buzzwords.

There are a few examples of this in the world of marketing. One of the biggest current examples of which is 'content marketing'. This is a large umbrella term, which has a huge number of different subsets. When people use the term content marketing, what do they actually mean? Blogging? On-Demand Videos? Live streaming? Creating slide decks? eBook creation? Designing infographics? You get the idea, there are so many options available.

There is absolutely no problem with the term 'content marketing' as far as I am concerned. We need these umbrella terms to help categorise. However, in isolation it doesn't add any meaning, depth or value. You need to be more specific in order to really add value to your audience, because the way in which you create, edit, share, repurpose and use videos is different to blog posts or infographics.

The way to avoid this negative sentiment is to be more specific. Using umbrella terms and phrases like 'how to do content marketing better' is just a wishy-washy statement that has no real meaning. Be more specific. 'How to create a live video series that shows your personality and adds value' – this is specific, and people know what they are getting out of it. Using a buzzword as a term to just get a few extra views, and not add value is a big part of why they can be perceived in a negative light.

The negative sentiment around buzzwords is in a number of cases warranted. However, one industry doesn't define a buzzword, and one buzzword doesn't define an industry.

Customer's don't care about your ROI (Return on Investment).
They just want great quality products and service.

- *Ash Phillips, YENA*

The Marketing Buzzword Podcast

FOUR

THE PSYCHOLOGY OF BUZZWORDS

T he psychology and rationale behind buzzwords is a particular fascination of mine, and one that from speaking to other people in business, other people are also interested in. In this chapter I'm going to take you on a dive into some of the psychological rationale behind the use of buzzwords, and the difference that can make to how the buzzword you have aligned yourself to is used. This will include dives into herd mentality, social transmission and tribal vocabularies. Let's get on with it then...

Herd Mentality

In all likelihood you will have heard the terms 'sheep mentality', 'herd mentality' or 'mob mentality'. They are all slight variations on the same idea, and ultimately look at how individual people are influenced by their peers or by a single person to adopt certain behaviours.

HERD MENTALITY DEFINITION:
THE TENDENCY OF PEOPLE TO BEHAVE IN THE SAME WAY AS
OTHERS WHO ARE SIMILAR TO THEM. THIS COULD BE

DRIVEN EITHER BY A SINGLE INDIVIDUAL OR BY A GROUP OF
INDIVIDUALS.

To give this definition some clarity and context here is an example I have thought up...

The idea is that you have a group of selectively bred dogs, sheep dogs. These dogs are the influencers and thought-leaders in a large field (a niche). In this field, there are loads of sheep (everyday marketers). They have their own personalities, thoughts, and just want to explore different parts of the field.

In this field the sheep dogs are the 'influencers', and they affect how and where the sheep move. Even a single influencer can have a significant impact upon the dynamics of a whole market, and the sheep/herd will react to you.

Taking this example and bringing it back to the real world, when you build authority around a niche topic, or buzzword, you are able to influence the marketers and business people in that area. When you do this by giving value and sharing knowledge, people will want to follow you and learn from you. This is you influencing the herd.

The amount of authority you have relates to how many marketers you can influence. That's where 'influencer marketing' is often done wrong. It's not about numbers of followers – it should never have been about the numbers. It's all about quality and authority.

It's for this very reason that you should be reading this book. Yes, a by-product of it will be building a large audience, but first and foremost it is about building authority, where people look to you for guidance. Remembering all the way though, that it's not just about you!

Tribal Vocabulary

Tribal vocabulary looks at how individuals such as academics, consultants and increasingly social influencers are driving tribalism in terms of using specific terminology to create almost private languages that resonate with a small subset of people.

It's this tribal language that causes the biggest divisions in terms of how people use and perceive jargon and buzzwords.

This is because of the assumption that whoever is reading the text or content is already familiar with the terms and phrases that you are subjecting the reader to. Or, even more worryingly, the problem of the author writing in a way that's so obscure, and so full of technical jargon without context, that even the most studious of readers can't apprehend it.

Those two issues are the primary drivers of the backlash against buzzwords. On a more positive note, this is fixable. It's not set-in-stone and as you'll see throughout the entirety of this book, it's possible to build a business off the back of a buzzword.

So, how do we overcome this? How do we as marketers trying to build our brands align ourselves to something that's quite clearly divisive and turn a buzzword into something we can own?

At a high level, a few words could suffice, and they go a bit like this: don't be that person that alienates his/her audience by not keeping things simple. Don't make readers have to work hard to understand you. KISS them – not literally – but by 'keeping it simple, stupid'. I'm not saying dumb things down, but write in a way that is easy to process and understand. If you want people to resonate with you and your content, you have to appeal to them, and reduce the number and size of your barriers to entry.

Buzzwords don't work and catch on when you don't introduce the idea and define the term to your audience. When you use buzzwords without introducing the idea and defining the

Why are we trying to build content? It's not to get a couple of likes. We should be building content to maintain our industry position and continue to grow. Grow our audience and our business profits. We should be helping our audience and giving them knowledge.

- Julia McCoy, Express Writers

The Marketing Buzzword Podcast

FIVE

REGIONAL AND CULTURAL EFFECTS ON BUZZWORDS

"Different cultures produce a different 'cool.' And your perception of 'cool' changes depending on where you are."

\- Labrinth

As a result of my podcast, I have been fortunate enough to be able to speak to amazing business and marketing brains from around the world about their experiences and views on certain buzzwords.

Something that really stood out to me from these conversations is how different countries, even regions, have different terms for the same thing. For any of us, it's really easy to become enveloped in our own little bubble of shared experiences with people that are like us, and move in the same circles as us.

Let's use the terms 'Thought-Leader', 'Influencer' and 'Key Opinion Leader'. These are three terms used widely, in

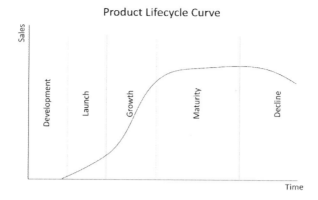

When changes happen, a small number of people are very visibly and vocally excited about it. These are the early adopters. These are the men and women, who share the potential, the uses and the initial trials and tribulations associated with the change.

During this time, a number of those early adopters will cease using the technology. This could be for a number of reasons such as technical issues, poor UI (user interface) or lack of clear practical applications (the options are pretty limitless really).

This drop off in usage is reflected in the downward slope after initial adoption. This is as true of buzzwords as it is of products. Following the drop off, there is usually a small plateau followed by a rise in usage.

This usually comes from the platform or the technology stabilising itself, coupled with users learning how to navigate and use the system better. This is the point at which buzzwords begin to take form and ultimately permeate into everyday use. This is completely dependent upon all other things being equal.

As time passes, the technologies, platforms and processes change and adapt. This is also very true of buzzwords. Right now chatbots are one of the hot topics, and they are very much in this growth phase, with lots of changes happening and still to come. As more and more people begin to adopt this technology and use this buzzword it begins to snowball.

This growth phase is extremely important. It's also the most volatile because there is so much going on, and both people and brands are struggling to learn, understand and master the buzzword in order to become an authority on the subject.

Following the growth stage, you reach maturity. This is where buzzwords begin to become a part of everyday vocabulary. At this stage, changes are less frequent, and both competition and usage are high.

If you want to stay at the leading edge, and at the forefront of things like social media, you have to be involved in working out how it works, teach people how to use it, and maximise its potential during the growth stage.

Although social media itself wouldn't be classed as a buzzword, because it is constantly evolving and changing, there is potential to become an authority in that field. You don't always have to jump on the newest and shiniest of words and terms. However, by looking to ride that wave of popularity from an early age, you are able to put yourself as THE person for knowledge and become part of how it builds, and when it reaches maturity, you have the credibility and consistency to be recognised as an authority.

In parts two and three, I share with those of you who have been involved with a buzzword from the outset, as well as the people who have got involved later on. Both ways can and do work, and only by staying at the forefront of change and providing ideas, examples, and by sharing your knowledge do you become synonymous with a buzzword, and thus become the authority your audience are looking for.

If your content isn't reflecting your brand and what you stand for. What is the point in you creating it?

- Andrew and Pete, Atomic

The Marketing Buzzword Podcast

SEVEN
DO WE REALLY NEED BUZZWORDS?

"Make everything as simple as possible, but not simpler."

— Albert Einstein

To buzzword or not to buzzword, that is the question. Unsurprisingly I fall on the 'to buzzword' side, however, there will still be many of you that argue otherwise.

That's good. I love a bit of healthy scepticism. Nevertheless, here are the reasons as to why I believe we still need buzzwords:

1) Buzzwords help organise and group content

Buzzwords can help us gather our thoughts, ideas and content. It allows us to have a central foundation or pillar upon which to base our creative efforts. By having a buzzword as your centre ground, you are able to build out a whole collection of associated, relevant content (think of your buzzword as a central supporting pillar). This is the basis for which parts two and three of this book are built upon. The idea of becoming synonymous by going deeper with your content and ideas.

2) Buzzwords get search volume

Buzzwords create a buzz (shocking right?). People want to know more and consume content that's based around it. Creating content that's heavily linked to the buzzword answers questions that people are asking, and offers them insights that they cannot get elsewhere; you are able to be found.

By doing this from the early days of a buzzword's existence, you are able to climb the search engine rankings quicker than you would with a crowded term, which is full of competitors, all vying for attention. As the buzzword increases in popularity, the number of searches does. If you consistently create valuable content around the buzzword, you will enhance your standing as a source of knowledge, and you guessed it, a subject authority.

If people are using a buzzword, they are searching for content about it, and they are looking for answers. Can you provide them?

3) Buzzwords show something new

Buzzwords are an indicator of progression. If there were no new buzzwords and new vocabulary, then it would be a sign that things are stagnant or receding. That is because buzzwords themselves are new things, not old. This could be new technologies, innovations, strategies or processes.

4) Buzzwords are evocative

Buzzwords elicit a response. Buzzwords by their very nature are designed, sometimes in a very clever and memorable way, to spark a thought, an idea or an emotion. They sometimes help us to paint a picture. They are enticing, and invite use. They help create a curiosity factor that makes us want to learn and explore. Without that sense of curiosity and desire, we wouldn't innovate, and wouldn't learn.

So yes, we do need buzzwords. Not necessarily all buzzwords, but we absolutely do need them.

Customer experience is kind of a big umbrella that covers all of the interactions with your customers.

- Joey Coleman, Joey Coleman

The Marketing Buzzword Podcast

EIGHT

WHAT IS THE FUTURE OF
BUZZWORDS?

"While intelligent people can often simplify the complex, a fool is more likely to complicate the simple."

— Henry David Thoreau

To close out this first section of the book, it's important that we look to the future.

Buzzwords are not going to go away. As far as I can see and predict they will always exist (feel free to come back to me in the years to come and tell me I'm right) because they will always be something new, something different, or changes within marketing.

Some people will always argue for their removal from the world (not even just business and marketing), but that's an ostrich mentality. Buzzwords are not just something that you can ignore and they will go away. Instead, as you'll see through parts two and three of the book, you need to embrace them, build your personal brand around them and build a business with them.

In the future, buzzwords will still be used differently across industry types. But, certain types will become less prevalent and others will become more so.

Buzzwords that are used currently as barriers, and used to create the 'superiority complex' that I've talked about will decrease in volume. This won't be for all industries, but most. This is because of increased customer power. They don't want to feel like they aren't being presented with all the facts, in a way that makes sense to them. After all, who can blame them, businesses have a history of lying and misrepresenting the facts. That's why we have advertising standards and quality standards.

As businesses when we use buzzwords in this way we are not instilling an atmosphere of trust and openness. Instead, we need to be clear and upfront with what things mean. We need to have a mind-set of, 'this is what... is, and this is how it can help you'.

In the UK we have something called the plain English campaign. This is a campaign which works with businesses, like those in financial services, to make things clearer for the customers and remove unnecessary jargon. It essentially sets out how businesses can write things and present content that is in layman's terms.

As I've already said, unnecessary jargon is the type of buzz-word that gives the rest a bad name. Both businesses, and customers have a role to play in the reduction of this jargon.

On the other side of the coin, we are going to see more of the type of buzzwords that we are focusing on in this book, the ones that are related to changes and events in the industry, ones that are related to technology and how we as marketers and business owners are adapting to an ever changing marketplace.

Buzzwords aren't evil, they aren't a symptom of laziness and they don't signify a lack of writing ability, when used properly.

Because there are so many changes in the marketing industry, buzzwords related to the industry will not go away, and in fact I predict that they will only increase in volume.

With all of that in mind, I am going to leave you with this: you can either embrace a buzzword, try and build an authority around it by sharing your own knowledge, expertise and advice consistently, over a period of time. Or, you can try and ignore them. You can try and imagine they're going to go away. You can use them in a way in which blocks people from the industry, and potentially create a negative perception of you and your brand.

Now it's time to put some meat on these bones and dive into 'how to build a personal brand using a marketing buzzword'.

People love to see what happens behind-the-scenes. It's a differentiator. When people and brands put out behind-the-scenes content it adds valuable information and offers a new dimension. It's a way to show your personality and create a connection.

- Nicole Osborne, Lollipop Social

The Marketing Buzzword Podcast

PART TWO
BUZZWORDS FOR PERSONAL BRANDING

Personal Branding. A buzzword in itself, but it's a word that doesn't just resonate with marketers or those in the business world, but people working in media, sport, politics and many other industries.

PERSONAL BRAND DEFINITION: THE CONSCIOUS AND INTENTIONAL EFFORT TO CREATE AND INFLUENCE PUBLIC PERCEPTION OF AN INDIVIDUAL BY POSITIONING THEM AS AN AUTHORITY IN THEIR INDUSTRY, ELEVATING THEIR CREDIBILITY, AND DIFFERENTIATING THEMSELVES FROM THE COMPETITION, TO ULTIMATELY ADVANCE THEIR CAREER, INCREASE THEIR CIRCLE OF INFLUENCE, AND HAVE A LARGER IMPACT.[1]

So, at the risk of making this book a bit like Inception by putting a buzzword within a buzzword within a buzzword, I want to look at how you, yes you, as a marketer, business owner or entrepreneur can build your own following, reputation and audience. This audience will grow and know you for something. A term, a word or a phrase that you have aligned yourself with and become one of the go-to experts on.

In this part of the book, I am going to look at how exactly you can do this, and dive deeper into a topic. So, hold on tight, we are about to explore how to build a personal brand around a marketing buzzword.

The concept of being human is great. But, it's not enough. You need some sort of strategy in order to make the most of social media and make more human connections. Otherwise you will spend all day talking and being social, but not actually growing your personal brand.

- Ai Addyson-Zhang, Classroom Without Walls

The Marketing Buzzword Podcast

NINE

SHOULD I COIN MY OWN, OR USE A BUZZWORD THAT ALREADY EXISTS?

"Successful ideas, they snowball."

- Ron Johnson

Before you can even begin to look at building an audience and a following around a buzzword, you have to actually find 'what your buzzword is'. For this you have two very distinct paths you can go down: coin your own, or use one that already exists.

"What's the difference?" I hear you ask. Fear not, let's separate out the paths.

Starting with coining your own term.

The point of coining your own term is that you are the first to use this particular word or phrase. This gives you a number of really key advantages over marketers and business people who are looking to get ahead and build their own audiences.

The first benefit of which is a term that we all learned back in business lessons in school, and it's something called 'first-mover advantage'. This is the idea that as a business, if you are first to market then you are able to capitalise on the lack of competition, and are therefore able to grow faster and quicker because of the lack of blockers in the market.

This 'first-mover advantage' is something that you, as an individual, can also capitalise on. You are able to coin your own term that no one else is using and take full advantage of all the space and freedom that you are afforded.

However, I would be lying to you if I said it was easy, and that you are about to walk into a field of dreams by coining your own term. Because, that is exactly not what it is. It is also very much not a case of 'build it and they will come'.

The flip side to this benefit of coining your own term is that this particular word or phrase has no existing following. It is likely not to be something that people are searching for, and it won't be something that people are already aware of. This means that you as the coiner of the term have to work very hard to build awareness of the term, especially if you have little-to-no existing audience or personal brand.

Despite the lack of initial audience that your given coined term may have, this could also be seen as a major benefit. This is the 'unique factor'. Marketers, business owners and entrepreneurs are crying out for ways in which to stand out and get noticed. Having a term that you can lay claim to and become associated with gives you a distinct advantage over anyone else in your industry.

Some common examples you'll see of terms that have been created in order to get noticed are: Mumpreneur (or mompreneur if you're American), Grandpreneur, Solopreneur and Dadpreneur. All spin offs from the word entrepreneur, but each designed to help individuals stand out and be noticed for something more specific than just an entrepreneur.

Another more complex example is the one of Mark Schaefer (https://businessesgrow.com) and his coining of the term 'content shock'. There was no existing audience, following, or even awareness that this was a thing, let alone that it had a name. Mark grasped this opportunity, and the rewards that came with it. 'Content shock' is now a widely known phrase in the content marketing world, and if you 'Google it' you will see Mark's name synonymous with it.

CONTENT SHOCK: A SITUATION WHERE CONTENT SUPPLY IS EXPONENTIALLY EXPLODING WHILE CONTENT DEMAND IS FLAT, DUE TO A FINITE ABILITY TO CONSUME ANY MORE CONTENT[1]

Make sure you take a look at Mark's original post on content shock from 2014. It was brilliant, and still is. It perfectly defines this term he has coined, and lays out why it's important and why people should care. A great example of coining your own term.

Another incredible example of coining a term of your own is by a man called Bryan Kramer. I've been a big fan and follower of Bryan for a number of years, specifically from the point that I was recommended his book: **There Is No B2B or B2c: It's Human to Human #H2H**[2]. As part of this book Bryan coined the term 'human to human' and an accompanying hashtag (#H2H).

Bryan Kramer Case Study

As it was just pointed out in the book, Bryan Kramer is the author of: *There Is No B2B or B2c: It's Human to*

Human #H2H, where he coined the term 'human-to-human'.

This term and this book had a profound impact on me as I began my journey into marketing. So, it was only natural for me writing about someone who has coined their own term, to ask Bryan how it came to be, how he maximised the potential it brought, and how he maintains the authority it gave him.

As you'll see from every case study I have included in this book, there are no overnight successes. They've had overnight success, but it was years in the making. Bryan's story is no different.

The first time Bryan really realised that this topic of H2H could catch on was when he gave a presentation at Bloomberg in San Francisco in front of a highly socialised audience. His message caught on, and within 48 hours of that conference tweets about Bryan's presentation had gathered over 128 million impressions (yes, that isn't a typo).

The way that the message resonated with the audience was the catalyst for Bryan to write the book. That book took just five days to write...

Although Bryan wrote the book in just 5 days, it had actually taken him years to research and plan. This involved countless hours of blog article writing. This helped Bryan really understand what he wanted to convey as soon as he started writing the book.

Before the book, Bryan had run a marketing agency for
13 years. This agency focused on humanising businesses in their marketing, and gave him the opportunity
to speak and present around the world. This platform
helped Bryan to grow not only his audience, but his
reputation as an industry authority.

In addition to speaking, Bryan spent years interviewing
people from leading brands across the world, including
a 1-on-1 video series with CMO's from the likes of
Oracle and Cisco. These activities, sustained over
years, helped give Bryan a platform upon which his
H2H message could resonate.

As word of H2H grew, Bryan quickly learned that his
idea divided opinions. People either loved the concept,
or hated it. The book helped to describe the term to the
masses, and validated its purpose, it was the ultimate
manifestation of his message. It was the ideal delivery
system to help Bryan get his message out there. It was
also the ideal medium in which to answer the question
that people kept asking "what is H2H?"

As time went on from the book launch, Bryan was
increasingly seen as a renowned expert on the topic of
human marketing. This status is one that can be hard to
maintain. Which is where my admiration for Bryan
increases further.
When I asked him how he maintained his 'expert
status', he simply told me that he doesn't think about it.
Instead, he thinks about how he can contribute next to
the community, and how he can help more.

I also love the way he embeds H2H in everything that he does. Everything that Bryan continues to do is an expansion on his previous work. I have seen this in action myself as a member of his Facebook group: Human Marketing Hub.

Since the book came out, so much has changed, but the principles remain the same, the definition remains the same. Bryan has continued his work on the pursuit of a human-centric approach to marketing. He is now much more strategic and leadership focused than marketing focused, but everything Bryan does is linked to H2H. That's the power of coining your own term.

Make sure that you take a look at Bryan's website for more details about H2H: https://www.bryankramer.com

What I love about Bryan's story is that not only has he built an incredible personal brand and become a true marketing authority since coining the term, he has also built a business (something covered in part three of this book). The fact that Bryan coined his own term meant he had the ability to control his own destiny, and build a successful career, with limited competition.

This is the power of coining your own. You can forge your own path. A path that you can stay on until the end, or not. The choice is there; you don't have to commit to it forever.

I'll address pivoting later on in this book in more detail, but for now it's really important that you understand that just because you start something, you don't have to push on with it forever.

On the other side of the coin to coining your own (pun fully intended), you need to look at whether you throw your lot in with an existing buzzword.

An existing buzzword is something that already exists in the wild, and is a term which someone else (either an individual or a company) is already using. In this event, you are looking to leverage the success and increasing awareness of this, in order to grow your own audience. Some examples would include: 'chatbots', 'influencer marketing', 'account based marketing' or 'customer experience'.

Before we go into the pros and cons of this, I want to make something very clear. You are not going to rip off content that already exists for this buzzword, because firstly, that's just not good practice, and secondly, that's not building authority, neither is it thought-leadership. That is copying!

Now that's cleared up, we can get started on the upside and downside. Because I'm a glass-half-full kind of guy, let's begin with a positive. The first major positive benefit of utilising an existing is that an audience already exists in some form for that buzzword, and people are now starting to organically search for that term.

This has a number of sub-benefits. Primarily, you are able to tap into an audience that already has an awareness of the term, has identified themselves as interested and are looking for more content. The secondary benefit to this is something known as the 'snowball effect'. Once that buzzword starts being used more, and growing in popularity, it will pick up more and more search traffic and interest.

SNOWBALL EFFECT: A SITUATION IN WHICH SOMETHING INCREASES IN SIZE, IMPORTANCE, SIGNIFICANCE OR INTENSITY AT A FASTER AND FASTER RATE. THIS USUALLY

BEGINS FROM SOMETHING VERY SMALL OR OF LITTLE SIGNIFICANCE.[3]

The hardest part is often getting started and building up those first few loyal and interested fans. Therefore, if you can find a term where the ball has started rolling, it can be much easier to pick up new fans for yourself.

Sticking with this snowball analogy, but coming from a slightly less positive viewpoint. If you are looking to leverage an existing term, you may be able to build up a small fan base relatively quickly because of the reasons just identified. However, as you try and pick up more 'followers' on this route, you will come up against other people doing the same. The people may or may not have already had significant first-mover advantage, this means you are competing to pick up the same potential audience. How should your potential audience choose which person to follow, because they haven't got time to follow everyone?

If you are treading the same path, one or both of you will struggle to pick up lots of these 'followers', so you have to differentiate. You have to find your own uniqueness and value proposition in order to pick up and grow your audience.

How late you are entering the race for followers or a buzzword, could help you decide whether it will be a worthwhile investment. This is because most of your potential audience have already been picked up by other 'thought-leaders' with their snowballs, and there may not be much left to pick up for yourself.

THOUGHT-LEADER: AN INDIVIDUAL OR A FIRM THAT IS RECOGNISED AS AN AUTHORITY IN A SPECIALISED AREA. THIS EXPERTISE IS OFTEN SOUGHT-AFTER BY THOSE WHO (https://www.experiencethisshow.com) with Joey Coleman.

As Dan's influence and authority continues to grow, I wanted to know how he did it, and how he kept on top of all the changes in his industry.

His answer was surprisingly simple: content creation and content curation.

This means not only sharing his own thoughts and ideas, but those of his peers and other authorities in the space. He does this because it helps build his own credibility and means that when he shares his own ideas people actually listen because he's not bombarding them with self-promotion.

I'm a big fan of Dan and his work. I love what he was talking about with social customer service, but his pivot also makes so much sense. The buzzword may have changed, but the theme remains the same.

There is a lot more to come from Dan, and I implore you to take a look at the work he is doing, and tell me it doesn't make total sense (because I don't think that's possible)!

Make sure you follow Dan on Twitter to see exactly what we've talked about in this case study: https://twitter.com/dgingiss

Although some buzzwords take longer than others to really

penetrate popular literature and vocabulary, you will be able to get an idea for the resonance and staying power that it is likely to have. If it will be a fad, then either look elsewhere or consider coining your own. This is because pivoting around buzzwords occasionally is OK, but pivoting on a regular basis can leave your audience confused, and that is not the way to build authority.

As someone who is looking to build a personal brand, knowing that there is an audience out there which will potentially buy into your messaging is crucial. This means you are not wasting your time and resources.

The problem with this though, is that you are slightly on the back foot, and being rather more reactive than proactive. Instead of building your thought-leadership and personal brand in an uncontested space, you are trying to compete directly with other people trying to build their own brands in this space. This isn't necessarily bad, because the market potential could be huge and, coming from a sporting background, I'm a huge believer that competition breeds improvement, but to not consider this would be foolish.

Do you have something that defines you and makes you stand out from everyone else vying to build an audience? Is this something that is unique to you? Ask yourself, 'why would people choose to listen to me over any other potential thought-leader?'

By identifying your strengths and your 'value proposition' as it's sometimes referred you are able to move from being on the back foot to the front foot.

As you can imagine, if a buzzword has been around for a little while and the competition is fierce, and you are creating bland, vanilla, beige content then you aren't going to go very far. Could you be the cooking estate agent? Could you be an

8os themed chatbot trainer? Keep reading for a case study on this.

Maybe you could be the person who teaches from the train if you get the train to and from work every day?

If you don't find something to help you stand out, you'll either:

1) not build an audience, or 2) lose your first-mover advantage to someone else who starts using the term you've identified.

In order for you to stand out, and not have to dive into niches within niches for your content to gain any small amount of traction, you have to... be bold. Wear your heart on your sleeve. Share your opinion. Present it in an engaging format that suits your personality. Be you. If you aren't rubbing a few people up the wrong way, then you aren't saying something different, you aren't being a thought-leader.

When you are deciding whether you want to coin your own term or not, it's important to do some research and identify gaps in the market, niches, and terms that are likely to grow in popularity.

You have to be selective, and you have to research. Just because you haven't heard the term before, it doesn't mean that it doesn't already exist. You also need to be careful of trademarks, as you don't want to find yourself stuck in some hot water because you have been building your personal brand around a term that's been legally given to someone else (the chances of this are pretty slim, but always worth checking).

TASK: IDENTIFY IF THERE IS A WORD OR TERM YOU USE OFTEN DURING YOUR WORK. IS THIS A WORD OR PHRASE THAT OTHER PEOPLE ALSO USE?
IF IT'S NOT, YOU HAVE FOUND YOUR NICHE. IF IT IS

ALREADY IN USE, HOW CAN YOU ADD YOU OWN UNIQUE
VALUE TO IT?

Jessika Phillips Case Study

I first heard of Jessika Phillips in about November 2017. Since then I've been a huge fan. She's taken the term 'relationship marketing' to new heights, and I see her as someone who doesn't just talk the talk, but walks the walk.

For Jessika it all started out from a job in corporate America at a Telecoms company, starting off in sales, progressing to management, then to distribution partner. In the last of those jobs Jessika was working with companies, helping them to sell the products of the business she worked for.

In order to do this well, she had to understand how those businesses sold and marketed themselves. She had to understand why, in a number of industries, people would choose to buy or work with smaller, more expensive businesses over large.

Jessika fell in love with the drive and passion that these businesses have, and the personal way in which these businesses operate. It was a world away from the corporate world that she was used to.

At a similar time, Jessika fell pregnant and became extremely unwell. Sick to the point that the company she was working for let her go. This meant that Jessika went from a high-flying career, earning 6-figures, and the breadwinner of her family to heavily pregnant and jobless.

As you can imagine, an extremely scary time. This massive change required equally large lifestyle changes. But, it also offered perspective. It gave Jessika the moment of clarity that many of us crave, yet often fail to receive.

This clarity helped Jessika to realise that she wanted to be able to help those smaller businesses that she had previously worked with. She saw so many things they were doing wrong, and knew she could help. There-fore, in 2010 she founded NOW Marketing Group. When she set this company up, she gave it a single purpose: 'to put relationships at the forefront of busi-ness and marketing'. Jessika wanted to build a company that stood for what she believed in, and to practice what she preached.

Since then, the company has grown considerably, and organically. Jessika has shown people and businesses that business could be done the opposite way to how they were always told. She put on free training sessions to get people through the door, then grew through referrals and word of mouth.

Over time, Jessika and her company properly systemised their approach (6 steps) to relationship marketing to make it highly contextual and easy to communicate. Jessika also gave it a name so that people could really understand it and buy into it: The Relationship Marketing System.

When I asked Jessika how she kept relevant and how she maintained her expert status (whether she saw it or not), she came back to me with two intriguing answers.

Firstly, on the topic of relevance; Jessika noted that her given term of 'relationship marketing' is one that has no physical boundaries. It is instead a philosophy and a way of being. It stays relevant because it can constantly be applied to new tools and systems. Therefore, the key to remaining relevant in terms of relationship marketing is to understand the new tools, and how to apply the philosophy to it.

She also noted that terms and ways of thinking that are entrenched in a thing, a channel, or a tool require a lot more pivoting. This is because they go out of fashion. She believes that a philosophy like relationship marketing holds up more much to the tests of time and technology.

The second thing that really intrigued me was that Jessika really doesn't see herself as an expert. She sees herself much more as an evangelist. She retains that love of learning and of serving. It's not about knowing it all, it's instead about being able to offer the most value to the people who want to listen.

This is how Jessika has been able to build not only a

successful business, but a successful personal brand alongside. To quote her: "I'm living my relationship truth". She feels so passionately about what she does, and what her business stands for, she is able to keep both intrinsically linked.

This true belief means that Jessika and her business can grow in tandem and the growth of her personal brand results in increased sales for NOW Marketing Group.

I'm a big fan of what Jessika and NOW Marketing Group (https://nowmarketinggroup.com) have done do-date, and I can't wait to see what's still to come!

	Pros	Cons
Coining your own buzzword	• Yours to own and build. • No direct competition. • You define it, and set the tone. • People instantly recognise you as the authority.	• Hard to gather momentum. • People have to be convinced. • No-one is already looking for the term.
Aligning yourself with an already existing buzzword	• People are already aware of the term, and are looking for more information and ideas around it. • Momentum already building.	• Higher levels of competition. • Less control over perception. • Harder to carve out your own niche.

Whether you decide to go down the route of coining your own, or aligning yourself to something that already exists, there are risks. But, there are also huge rewards.

You need to choose your own path. The choice is all yours. You can either take the road that's well travelled and already built, or take the scenic route where the path is unknown, but area is untouched and unspoilt. Which path will you choose?

audience buying into this buzzword is essential. Much like how adding context gives clarity to the initial question 'is this relevant to me?' Examples, case studies and demonstrations provide the evidence to show that the buzzword can be applied in a range of business types, in different industries with different sized head counts and different structures.

Remember that it is not only the here and now which is important, but the medium and long-term value proposition.

Rightly so, people are not willing to invest large amounts of time or money on things which are only going to have a small short-term return. In some cases, your given buzzword may be about the short term. This is fine, as long as it is made clear to your audience. Don't try to dupe people. You will get found out. However, I've found that in 90%+ cases, a buzzword when used properly can have a lasting impact on a business not just a short-term gain.

To put this into context for you (because I want to practice what I preach). Chatbots were a big deal in 2018. It's important for you as someone who wants to become an industry authority on chatbots to help people understand what they are, how to use them and the benefits they will bring (both now and in the future). Some examples of businesses using chatbots include: KLM, Whole Foods and TechCrunch. They are using chatbots embedded into their websites and social media platforms like Facebook Messenger to great effect.

For you as a budding authority to be able to show used cases from different industries with different styles is a big win. You need to be able to demonstrate how other brands are investing in this technology as a way for them to improve their businesses.

Over time, you will start building a back catalogue of high quality, relevant content around a word or phrase. This is the cornerstone to your success in becoming an authority, because it shows consistency over time, and demonstrates continuous value. It will give you organic credibility and show that you are the person who can help.

It comes back to the phrase, 'like, know, trust'. When you break down a term and start to help people, they begin to like you. The more you engage and speak with them the more they get to know you, and the value you can bring. The more value you can give them (over time) the more they will come to trust you.

Social selling isn't just a term. It's a collection of tactics and strategies.

- Nicky Kriel, Nicky Kriel

The Marketing Buzzword Podcast

ELEVEN

A PERSONAL BRAND HAS PERSONALITY

"A great personal brand shows off your expertise in addition to your personality. If you err on the side of only showing expertise, you may appear knowledgeable, but audiences won't understand why they will enjoy working with you. If you only show personality without expertise, they might like you but won't know what special skills you bring to the table."

- Greg Kihlstrom, Yes Agency

Personality is especially important if you are trying to break into an established market. And, if you are going down the route of coining your own term, you will only see its importance rise over time (so you will be glad you started adding personality into your content from the outset).

One of the biggest differentiators between you and your competitors is... you. You are unique, and are able to relate to a

If we spent all of our time creating bland, vanilla content, that is the same as everyone else's, then there is really no point in content marketing.

- *Andrew and Pete, Atomic*

The Marketing Buzzword Podcast

TWELVE

HOW TO BECOME THE TEACHER THAT YOUR BUZZWORD NEEDS

"Always do what you believe to be best for your students. They should always be your number one priority. Think, how does this benefit my students? If that question is difficult to answer, you may want to reconsider"

- Derrick Meador, ThoughtCo

I n order for you to be recognised as the industry authority on your chosen buzzword you have to become the teacher. In this chapter, we are going to explore exactly how you can become the authority your buzzword needs, and how you can become the go-to person associated with that buzzword.

The first thing you need to be extremely clear on when you are setting out your stall as a teacher of your buzzword is... **it is not about you**. It should never be about you. When you are looking to build your personal brand you need to be as transparent as possible to show why people should follow you. What is the value proposition for them? What will they get from you and your teachings? Will they be able to apply it to their business?

The worst talks, podcasts and blogs I read are essentially self-promotional mumbo jumbo, full of how they (the author/speaker) helped every business they've ever talked to make more money than ever before. You know the ones. We've all experienced them before. Don't be that guy. Don't be the value sucker, be the value giver.

How many of those blogs, podcasts and talks have you wanted to engage with again? How many have you recommended to a peer? I'm going to take a punt and say virtually none. Likely none at all. Why? Because it was all about them and not about you.

Yes, it's great using case studies and examples in your teachings, because as we established at the beginning of this section, context is king. But, banging your own drum isn't the way to build authority.

In order to establish yourself as a teacher, you have to go right back to the start. You have to understand where the baseline knowledge is for your audience.

If you've decided to coin your own term then, it's pretty safe to say that your baseline should be pretty damn close, if not, square at o. If you are going to make a push into a clearly established term like 'guerrilla marketing' then you may be able to start from a higher level, but it's always good to cover the fundamentals first.

{Hint: The lower the starting point the better. It gives you more content, more time and more social proof. Also helps validate your ideas and ensure your audience all have a similar understanding}

Some baseline questions you should look to cover include:

"What is ....?" Is ...... applicable to all industries?" "What are some of the key principles surrounding ....?"

Once you get your baseline established and your audience on the same level, you will be able to begin really educating your audience and building a following. You need to remember that people will find you and your buzzword at different stages of both their personal and business journeys, therefore it's vital that you create content appropriate and valuable for them.

It's also important that you create content that fits with their POV (point of view). This is something I've taken to call 'framal learning' (have I just coined a buzzword?), and essentially means framing things from the audience's viewpoint. It's really linked back to context. To become the authority on a given buzzword you must understand, I mean really understand what your audience want to get out of the valuable time spent reading, watching and listening to your teachings.

FRAMAL LEARNING: THE PROCESS OF ADDING CONTEXT
AND ADDING REFERENCE POINTS TO LEARNING OUTCOMES
TO ENABLE STUDENTS TO UNDERSTAND THE REASONING FOR
THE LEARNING OUTCOMES EXISTENCE.

For many of you reading this, you won't consider yourself a teacher. That's OK. However, if you want to become the marketing authority for your buzzword, you are going to have to teach. You can't develop thought-leadership without it.

One of the first things you need to know before you begin teaching is what sort of teacher you want to be and how you want to teach.

1. **Teacher-centred**

A teacher-centred approach is one where the teacher/lecturer places themselves squarely in the role of subject matter expert, and is seen as an authority by the learners. In this approach, the learners are expected to be passive, but receptive. They are expected to sit, listen and digest all of the information given to them.

This method doesn't use much, if any, learner/teacher interaction, and is an example of most lectures and conference talks. It's a very closed style which doesn't leave much room for widening the thought process, but does keep the content and lesson highly focused.

2) **Learner-centred**

In a learner-centred approach, teachers are learners at the same time. The idea is that the teacher looks to play a dual role in the room to extend 'intellectual horizons'. It comes back to the teacher understanding that they may not know it all, and that by engaging with the class, they are not only improving the class' knowledge, but also their own.

In this method, the teacher is a resource of information, and encourages their class to widen their own knowledge through idea sharing and learning through discussion. They are a facilitator.

3) **Content-focused**

A content-focused approach means that both teachers and learners are led by the content itself, often in the form of case studies and examples. This method looks at providing highly contextualised knowledge and skills that fit perfectly with the content at the heart of the approach. The emphasis is laid on clarity, analysis and giving context to both the teachers and the learner.

Both learners and teachers are able to build highly specific skills. However, this method can be too focused and may ignore important skills that aren't relevant to the content used. It's highly impactful, but limited.

4) Interactive/participatory-centred

An interactive/participatory method borrows elements from all three of the above (without leaning specifically on either the teacher, learner or content). This method requires a high degree of situational awareness, and requires the teachers, learners and content to adapt to their surroundings and environment (i.e. stock exchange and financial crisis or Facebook Groups and changing Facebook algorithms). Both the teachers and learners have to adapt to make sure that the learnings are appropriate to the situation and the learners are required to understand the importance of the situation and why learning in that environment is relevant and beneficial.

Ultimately, there is no right or wrong method. There is no one-size-fits-all approach. It is dependent on how you feel most comfortable, and the type and range of learners you have in front of you. It is also important to remember that for learners, there also isn't one method to rule them all. Some will like different methods at different times, for different examples in their learning journey. That's ok. You just have to judge what is most appropriate and when. Also, what style you are most comfortable with yourself, because if you aren't able to effectively teach then you can't give them the value they need/want.

TASK: IDENTIFY WHICH LEARNING STYLE BEST SUITS YOUR TEACHING STYLE. WHICH METHOD DO YOU FEEL YOU CAN PROVIDE THE MOST VALUE TO YOUR AUDIENCE?

In addition to the different teaching methods, there are some learning styles you should be aware of.

By understanding how your potential audience are wanting to learn, you are putting yourself in the best possible position to help them develop and become the marketing authority they are looking for.

There are four main learning styles that you need to be aware of (there are more, but we are going to stick with the main ones).

Visual (Sight)

Auditory (Sound)

Verbal (Linguistic)

Kinaesthetic (Physical)

People learn and retain information in a variety of ways. Therefore, it's vital that you appeal to as many of them as possible, by providing them with a number of channels and opportunities to be able to absorb the valuable information you are providing.

So, how can you appeal to learners that prefer different learning styles?

Visual learners

In order to engage with visual learners, you need to consider how your content appeals to their eyes. This means creating pictures, videos, and content that has colours and patterns in order to provide stimulus to their visual senses.

Auditory learners

For auditory learners, sound is key. When you are teaching people about your buzzword, consider the use of sounds as cues. Think about the pitch of your voice when you are speaking (are you emphasising the key ideas?). In your videos and podcasts, consider thinking about how you can use sound to convey when something is important. You can also think about sounds for increasing tension, anticipation, and drama.

Verbal learners

Verbal learners are arguably one of the hardest to get the balance right for. Especially if you prefer the 'teacher-centred' approach in how you communicate your knowledge on your given buzzword. With this learning style, you need to encourage conversations and dialogue. You help them learn by allowing them to frame things from their own point-of-view.

With this method you have to be open to being questioned, and have your views challenged. Some of the best examples I see of this learning style in action is with Facebook Live Interviews and conversations. In these, viewers get an opportunity to openly question the interviewer or interviewee to extract the knowledge they want/need to know instead of just being told the information the interviewer/interviewee wants them to know.

Although this can be a tricky learning style, I have found it to be one that allows both the audience and the 'marketing authority' to learn off each other, and truly demonstrate knowledge on a subject, while in tandem helping the audience frame the buzzword in a way that makes absolute sense for them.

Kinaesthetic learners

Kinaesthetic learning is a style that isn't particularly easy to communicate, especially when so much more of our learning comes from digital channels. However, when it comes to live events, workshops and conferences, the people who best fit this style can learn a huge amount. This is because it requires some sort of physical stimulus. They like learning in the form of activities, demonstrations and having a hands-on approach.

This is not something that's easily done. But, what you can do is give learners an example scenario and ask them to put it into their frame of reference, and create a campaign, project, or solution. This will allow them to practically apply what they know and understand how the different pieces of the puzzle fit together.

It is possible to appeal to these people through digital channels, however, it isn't very easy.

TASK: THINK OF SOMETHING YOU CAN DO TO REACH LEARNERS OF DIFFERENT STYLES. HOW CAN YOU TEACH THEM IN A STYLE THAT SUITS THEM? WHAT CONTENT CAN YOU CREATE THAT RESONATES WITH MULTIPLE LEARNING STYLES?

Whichever teaching and learning styles you decide to focus on, and make use of, you must convey value to your audience, and you must be comfortable doing it in that way. You must stay true to yourself and your ideals, and you have to communicate in a way in which you enjoy teaching. If you are faking it and forcing it, it will show. Enthusiasm, raw enthusiasm, cannot be falsified.

When you are passionate about something, and you let it show, people will sit up and listen. Think about some of your favourite speakers, teachers and practitioners, would you say they were passionate about their subject? I'd put a wager down for 'heck yes'. You follow those people because they love what they do, and you keep coming back, because they are entertaining you and teaching you.

When you are using any of your given mediums to communicate, you have to put in 100% every time. I mean literally every single time. If you aren't putting in everything that you have, it will show. Take podcasting for example. People can't see you, they can't physically interact with you. They are also likely multitasking while listening to you. Therefore, if you want to grab their attention, you have to be attention worthy.

At the end of this book, that is the person I want you to be: someone who loves what they do, and feels strongly that the word or phrase they've aligned themselves to is important for people to know. And, most importantly, I want you to be the teacher that your audience wants to learn from.

In order to wrap up this chapter properly, it would be amiss of me not to mention feedback. As a teacher, and someone who is looking to build a personal brand around a buzzword, you absolutely must get, and act upon feedback.

Feedback is your audience's way of telling you they care about what you are trying to communicate. When people are time poor and surrounded by distractions, the fact that they have taken the time to tell you is a big deal. Especially when they don't have to, and when they have so many other things to spend their precious time on.

Feedback is your way of being able to understand what others see when they look at you and your content. Don't dismiss it because you don't necessarily agree, because they are your target audience, and those are the people you want your messages to resonate with.

I implore you to ask for as much feedback as possible, as often as possible. By showing that you care, and that you are listening, you are going to reap the rewards. That is because a personal brand is based on you, everything about you. The way you walk, the way you talk, look, listen, interact, smell and the vibe you give off.

The more you are showing your audience that it is all about them and that they are at the forefront of your mind and your teachings, the faster your audience will grow, and the sooner you will become recognised as a marketing authority for your given buzzword.

Always remember, that as you build your personal brand, and teach people about your given buzzword; it is never about you (hopefully you have been noticing the theme).

Meaningful interactions aren't just single, small comments. It's about longer, more detailed comments and conversations. We need to social media more social again.

- Christine Gritmon, Christine Gritmon Inc

The Marketing Buzzword Podcast

THIRTEEN

WHERE ARE YOU GOING TO PLANT YOUR FLAG?

"Online, there is a lot to do if you want to be successful... And with the huge amount of channels available, it's just not realistic to try be everywhere at once, even with automation"
- Sian Lloyd, Rebrnadly

T his chapter is going to explore 'the where'. In particular, the channels you are going to build your authority in, and the mediums you are going to use to create your content. There are a number of factors that come into play when making decisions about both of these areas.

Starting with the channel (where people are going to find your content), you must always consider where your audience are already. Are they on Instagram? Twitter? Medium? Facebook? Quora? There is absolutely no point trying to target a platform that has no or little relevance to your audience. Likewise, you also shouldn't try and take an omni-channel approach and target every single channel you think that your audience may use.

I've found that a multi-channel approach is what generally works best (although there are exceptions). This would mean utilising two or three channels at any given time. Enough to reach a large cross-section of your potential audience, but not enough so that you are stretched too thin and lose the ability to add as much value in each channel as possible.

This doesn't mean you have to split your time evenly across all three. You can prioritise, and you should test. See where your audience interacts most, and where the engagement is best. By using multiple channels, you are able to test what works, what doesn't, and you are able to quantify it.

I'm going to use my friend John Espirian (https://espirian. co.uk) as an example here. He is the 'relentlessly helpful technical copywriter'. His main focus in terms of channels is LinkedIn, but he is also pretty active on Twitter. This activity allows him to engage with audiences on either channel, and thus further his reach. That being said John's focus is on LinkedIn, for him it's a much better channel for growing his business, and having meaningful conversations. But, he maintains his Twitter to help his personal brand and reach people who he may not be connected with on LinkedIn. Although his primary focus is on LinkedIn, it is definitely enhanced by using both.

That being said, there is merit in the 'go all-in on one channel approach'. I can totally see how dedicating your time and resources into making one thing successful will pay off. However, from what I've seen and the vast majority of people that I have featured in this book, the one channel approach isn't the norm, and for good reason.

At least having a presence on other channels allows you to

be open to new opportunities and possibilities whenever they arise. Even if you are unable to use them as much as you like.

If you don't have a presence you're at ground zero, and it's a long, long way to climb to become a recognised authority. It's not impossible, by any stretch, but you are restricting yourself.

Whether you decide on a single, multi or omni-channel approach, you have to be able to commit to it. You have to be consistent, and you have to think long-term. I am a big believer that consistency is the core of a personal brand, and it's the reason I focus specifically on two channels daily (Twitter and LinkedIn) and a few other channels on a more adhoc basis (Facebook, Instagram and YouTube).

The reason I describe consistency as being at the core of a personal brand is that you can have some interesting thoughts and ideas, maybe even do a few really cool videos. However, it's the ability to do this consistently, over time that makes the difference between you becoming a real marketing authority, or a flash-in-the-pan marketer.

If you cannot deliver quality, insightful and valuable content about your given buzzword on a regular basis then how can you expect your audience to come back to you on a regular basis? Trust is a two-way street. You have to build trust by consistently adding value to their lives, and they will reward you with trust in kind, which will lead to views, shares, sales and talks.

When you are considering the space in which you want to plant your flag, you must think about whether that is an owned space, or a loaned space. By that I mean, do you own the space (i.e. website, emails and direct mail) or the loan the space (social media sites, blogging platforms like medium and influencer marketing). These are essentially spaces where you are creating on platforms owned by others, and have no real control over any changes that they make to the platform.

Ideally you want to build on an owned space. This is because it is yours. You own it, you dictate what happens next, and how you use the data that you've obtained (within the confines of the law). You also decide upon what features to present, how you showcase your content, and anything else you are physically capable of doing.

It is possible to use both owned and loaned spaces, you don't have to choose one or the other. But, you need to have a central repository where your audience can find all your content, ideas and connect with you. You need to have central space where you can direct all your traffic. This is often a web page, but could equally be a Facebook Page or Instagram Profile. In most cases, this is the place you are most active, or the area you are most likely to get your audience to take action, either book you as a speaker, sign up to your course, or buy your services.

In the following case study, I present to you Mark Masters, a man who I have known for a number of years. He is doing exactly as I set out, and it's brilliant.

Mark Masters Case Study

It all started with an email. Yes, an email. That email started in October 2013, and every week since then Mark Masters has sent out his coveted 'You Are The Media' weekly email.

Before the first email Mark was blogging, since January 2012, which as we all know is great, but he felt some-

thing was missing. He needed something to share with
his clients and prospects. Something that would be
useful and insightful. This also had the secondary
benefit of helping Mark to stop spending money on
promotional activity to be top of mind. All of which
were just expensive and short-lived. This wasn't what
Mark wanted, hence his commitment to a personalised,
long-term medium.

Very much by his own admission, Mark says his first
few emails were "rubbish" (but in fairness, what isn't
rubbish when we look with the benefit of hindsight?).
They were plain, and generic, but they were always
done with the right intent. It has helped Mark to build
a 2,500+ strong subscribed email list (post-GDPR).
Now, some of you may think that 2,500 isn't that much,
but remember that it's quality over quantity. If like
Mark, you are to have over 2,500 opted-in, highly relevant subscribers, you are doing something very right.

Although Mark's staple was and still is the email, since
2016 he began to build additional structures on top of
this solid foundation. This includes the development of
localised lunchtime meet-ups called 'You Are The
Media Lunch Club'. These lunch clubs take Mark's
relationships with his email subscribers to another
level, a physical level. They are about advancing
learning and building familiarity. This in turn leads to
trust and familiarity with those who are part of the You
Are The Media community.

Mark has subsequently taken these lunch clubs to

another level again, by introducing the monthly 'You Are The Media Podcast' and by organising the 'You Are The Media Conference'. I was lucky enough to be at its inauguration in 2018, and can truly testament to the community that Mark has built. The conference is the culmination of Mark's commitment to building a loyal audience over the space of years, not weeks or months.

When I was talking to Mark for this case study I was amazed to hear how he will for as long as he can see, keep on with his weekly emails. In fact, he described them as "his heartbeat", it has a regular rhythm. They are what gives life to every other piece of activity from the You Are The Media network.

Not only has Mark been building on top of his emails with more owned spaces, he's also begun leveraging the power of loaned spaces. Mark is a believer of building a home base ie.your website, but taking from places that are not yours ie. social media.

OWNED MARKETING SPACE DEFINITION: A MARKETING CHANNEL THAT IS OWNED BY THE INDIVIDUAL OR BUSINESS THAT IS USING IT. THIS REQUIRES THE BUSINESS OR INDIVIDUAL TO HAVE PURCHASED OR BUILT THE CHANNEL THEMSELVES.

LOANED MARKETING SPACE DEFINITION: A MARKETING CHANNEL WHICH IS USED BY AN INDIVIDUAL OR A BUSINESS, BUT IS NOT OWNED BY IT. THESE SPACES COULD BE FREE-TO-USE OR RENTED.

They are owned and controlled by an external business or organisation.

This relates to taking advantage of what is readily available ie. free, but have an objective to bring people back to you. For instance, if you subscribe to updates from a social channel, you are in danger of becoming a needle in a haystack. You can still create a centre of gravity ie. your website, but in order to get people to commit and spend time, it is also worthwhile for people to see a level of consistency in other places.

Mark's formula works like this with the balance between owned and loaned:

1. Build a presence where you are confident that your message is not the same as everyone else and you can house the blogging, the video and the audio (your website)

2. Transfer a strand of that narrative to any channel where the audience already exists, such as a micro story (a post with up to 1,300 characters) on LinkedIn.

3. Pull people away so they can see that the party is happening at yours. This helps build a stronger subscribed audience that is 100% yours.

In recent times, Mark like many other business owners has had to pivot. Although his weekly emails are still extremely valuable, he introduced a Facebook Group to

Slideshares

These mediums are just the tip of the iceberg, and many can be used across a variety of channels (the space(s) you are going to look to build your personal brand in). Each of these mediums requires a slightly different skill set, and it is impossible to become a master at all of them. Not least because they are evolving and adapting so quickly. However, you are able to do and use a number of them concurrently. Only by actually doing it will you really know if it's something you can do over the medium and long term.

This next case study features a guy called Andrew Davis. He's a man I look up to immensely in terms of video marketing. He's smashing it with his given industry, and I hope by including this case study, you might feel a bit inspired too.

Andrew Davis Case Study

Andrew Davis is a man who I have so much time for. He's making an incredible contribution to the world of marketing through the medium of video. His work has seen him speak on stages across the world; if you want to know about video marketing, he is your guy.

When I spoke to Andrew about where it all started, he told me that it feels like video is in his DNA. His passion started with working as a childhood actor, continued through attending university in Boston, and remained as he worked for TV on programmes like NBC's Today Show, The Muppets and Sesame Street.

During this time, Andrew saw the power of entertainment, and the way that both could be combined to incredible effect. Entertainment has the power to make people love, to question and to learn.

Star Wars, Barbie, Paw Patrol and Dr Who are all incredible examples of films and TV shows that have had incredible success away from their original medium. This includes merchandising, spin-offs and computer games. That's the power of marketing and entertainment.

In 2001 Andrew made the full switch over to marketing, where he ran his agency with his business partner until 2012 (no mean feat). Into this agency Andrew poured his love and experiences from TV to help businesses tell a visual story, that their customers would embrace and love.

Because of their experiences within the TV industry, they were able to offer something a bit different to traditional marketing agencies, and quickly found that businesses had a real interest in the power of video.

Today, in post-agency life, Andrew continues to create amazing videos. So, I had to ask him one question . . . how on earth do you stay relevant and on top of your game? His answer was simple, "aeration – aerate your ideas as often as possible with people". It's such a simple thing to do to, literally a tweet could be all you need. You need to find out if you are going to strike a chord with people.

What Andrew also stresses is the need for repeatability. He is constantly asking the question: how can this be repeatable, and not a one-off, or a one-hit-wonder?

He shares two really important ways of building repeatable content. Firstly, plan, not just one step ahead, but three, four, five. Stay ahead of the curve. And, secondly, test. Test first, and test early. That helps give Andrew the confidence that the content and the idea is sound.

I think that Andrew is an expert in the world of video marketing. I have no doubts at all. But, when I asked him about how he maintains this expert status, he was adamant that he wasn't. Instead he called himself an investigator.

He says that it's his curiosity that has kept him relevant. He's always learning, always adapting, and always aerating. He quite openly says, he does not have all the answers.

For me, this is what makes Andrew awesome, and I really hope you think so too!

Make sure you take a look at his website, and in particular watch the videos. This guy is a genius: https://www.akadrewdavis.com

Andrew is an awesome person to be able to include in this book. However, I wholly understand that some of you may not have such a love for a medium from the off, and that it may take time for you to enjoy. So, my question to you; do you think you will feel more comfortable using a medium the more you do it? It's important to know that you may not feel at home right away with every medium you try. I know very well from experience. It took quite a while (I'm talking months) for me to feel at home with podcasting. Now I love it, at first I didn't. I'm so glad that I pushed through, and now I'm very comfortable with it (my voice still doesn't sound like I think it does in my own head though).

You need to use a medium that you can feel comfortable in. It may take time, but if you are honest with yourself you will know whether you enjoy it or not, and you will grow into it.

Chris Strub (https://www.teamstrub.com), the man who wrote the foreword to this book, is someone I have so much admiration for in this regard. He is building a Facebook community around video (Social with Strub), and encouraging people to take that step. As a part of this community I can see the changes in people, and see how much more confident they look and sound on camera. It's frankly amazing. He's also built an online course off the back of it (https://academy. teamstrub.com/). This course is equally brilliant, and really helps his audience to build confidence and understand the potential video could have for them, across a range of mediums.

What I find most amazing though is that Chris doesn't just teach, he lives and breathes video on social. He builds connections, shares values, tests ideas and encourages conversations. He does some videos alone, and he does some with others. His primary channel is Twitter, but slowly, over time, he is expanding his reach using a multi-channel approach. The time and care he takes in the relationships he builds is astonishing. In the channel of Twitter, using the medium of live video, I can think of no-one better!

Not only do you have to be comfortable creating content

using a particular medium, you also have to be able to effectively teach your audience using it. That isn't always easy, and you have to remember 'as a teacher, it's not about you'.

If you are going to build an audience, your content has to be shared in a way that they can understand. Content for the sake of content doesn't add value. If you aren't able to effectively help your customers in that medium, then it may be worth looking at an alternative.

I have tried a number of different content mediums over the years, and through lots of trial and error, I have found a few mediums that I believe are right for me and my audience. I rank them in order of preference looking at how comfortable I am, how effectively I can teach in the medium, and how much value my audience will get.

1 - Speaking
2 - Podcasting
3 - Videos
4 - Blog

TASK: MAKE A TABLE OF ALL THE POTENTIAL CONTENT TYPES YOU MAY WANT TO USE.
SCORE ON A SCALE OF 1-5 HOW COMFORTABLE YOU FEEL USING THAT MEDIUM.
SCORE ON A SCALE OF 1-5 HOW EFFECTIVELY YOU THINK YOU CAN TEACH PEOPLE IN THAT MEDIUM.

Those mediums work for me, and they may work for you. My strengths do not lie in creative infographic creation, memes, cartoons and consistent micro-blogging. Those are things that I am not completely comfortable with, and cannot effectively teach in, so I avoid them, or, when needed, outsource them.

With videos, I am not overly comfortable. I am able to do

them, but I'm by no means a natural (it's getting there though with practice), however my audience find them valuable and I can teach effectively in that medium. Therefore, I do video. As a teacher and someone who is looking to continually build my own authority, I have to put my audience first.

Podcasting and speaking are my two preferred mediums, and they also seem to resonate with my audience. I didn't know this straight away. It took time to find my mediums, but now I'm able to create content that adds value, and I love doing it!

Before you begin creating content in your chosen space, with your preferred medium(s), you should be considering how competitive your market is with other people vying for your audience's attention. This doesn't mean you shouldn't use that medium, but you may have to work harder, smarter, and do more to stand out.

You have a choice. You can be first, you can be better, or you can be different. Or, even better, be all three!

In some areas such as 'marketing strategy' there is a lot of competition, across a wide range of channels and mediums. However, by coining your own term, either within the overarching theme of marketing strategy, or just something completely unique, you can position yourself as a marketing authority. By being first to market with your buzzword in the spaces you want to be in using a medium you can dominate, and teach in, you are going to build your audience and authority.

When you are looking to leverage an existing buzzword you have to work harder, and work smarter, because the competition is a lot greater. In this case it's even more important than ever to build a rapport quickly with your potential audience. Kelly Noble Mirabella has done this amazingly by leveraging the power of Facebook Live and YouTube primarily to build a personal brand around the buzzword 'chatbots'. She has built such an engaged fan base, who love getting to know her, are fans of the way she presents, and ultimately want to know more about chatbots. She is quickly becoming an authority in this space, and they are blowing their competitors apart.

Kelly Noble Mirabella Case Study

Kelly Noble Mirabella is smashing it in the world of chatbots. She's building an audience and a reputation based upon a technology and buzzword that's on so many marketers' lips.

For Kelly, 2016 was the year that chatbots came onto her radar. It came in the form of a Facebook ad; this ad turned out to be a chatbot. In this ad, the company asked their audience to comment below to receive an instant message with an offer. And, shockingly, it worked.

The funny thing about this chatbot though, is that it was really simple. But, Kelly saw the potential that chatbots could offer.

It wasn't until Social Media Marketing World in 2017 where Kelly saw Molly Mahoney talk about "how to maximise the opportunities of Facebook Live", did she really start thinking about the possibilities chatbots could offer.

Over the next 6+ months Kelly begun watching and

following the world of chatbots. She admittedly became obsessed, watching hours, and hours YouTube videos. Whilst doing that, she noticed a few things:

1. A lot of the videos were really poor quality
2. Many were too long and boring
3. There weren't many videos focused on ManyChat as a platform.

Naturally, there was one conclusion. Kelly decided to do it herself; better, and different to everyone else. In order for her to do really get this right, she hired two of the best in the business; Andrew and Pete as her brand coaches.

This coaching resulted in a really cool, and unique feel to Kelly's videos. 80s themed videos, jam-packed full of useful info, in a way that way fun and engaging, not just a screen recording.

Social Media Marketing World 2018 was the next big point of reference for Kelly and her growing personal brand and reputation. She improved her consistency and she improved her presentation style. She began looking at specific types and models, working out their intricacies and sharing her findings.

This new strategy helped her audience to grow from 90 YouTube subscribers to over 900 in just 6 months.

In addition to creating YouTube videos, Kelly also spread her wings into other mediums. She became incredibly active in the Manychat Facebook group. Not creating spammy content, about her YouTube channel, but being actually helpful. Asking questions, answering them and providing opinions and insights.

Kelly's aim is simple; be really helpful. She doesn't very herself as an expert on chatbots, but as a student. Through her speaking, videos and coaching, she wants to help people get to grips with chatbots in a fun, easy-to-understand and to-the-point manner.

What I love about what Kelly is doing, is that she is truly embracing the "it's not about you, it's about them mentality". She learns, then she teaches. And, her aim is to always teach you in a better way than she had to learn herself.

I absolutely love that attitude, and it's exactly why she has such a growing reputation as an authority within the chatbot community. I have no doubt though, that this is just the start.

Make sure that you take a look at Kelly's website (https://stellarmediamarketing.com), and Youtube channel (https://www.youtube.com/user/stellar247) you'll see why I love what she is doing so much.

Whether or not your given market is highly competitive or not, you should always be looking to innovate and do something differently, just like Kelly. However, it shouldn't be a case of innovating for innovation's sake. I want you to work smarter, and be considered in your approach.

Think of building a personal brand like a game of chess. You are in control over your own side (i.e. personal brand). You need to make sure that the moves you make define you, and not the moves your opposition makes. You need to think a few moves ahead. The smarter you work, the more pieces you will have left on the board and the more likely it is for your personal brand to win over your competitors.

It sounds easy right? It's not. I would absolutely love to say it was, but you'd quickly call me out for BS (rightly so too).

That's because as much as you control, there are opposite forces at play. This includes your competitors and the market in which you are building your brand. You have to make choices. These choices will define you, so you have to consider everything from the buzzword you choose, to the medium you use. So, what is your flag, and where are you going to plant it?

Anybody can create content. But, what does it actually mean? If the content you create isn't aligned with what you stand for, it is meaningless. Great content aligns with what you stand for and adds value to someone's life.

- *Mark Masters, The ID Group & You Are The Media Community*

The Marketing Buzzword Podcast

FOURTEEN
DON'T JUST SCRATCH THE SURFACE, DIG DEEPER

"Never become so much of an expert that you stop gaining expertise. View life as a continuous learning experience."

- Denis Waitley

In this chapter I want to break down how you forge longer lasting relationships with your audience. I want you to really think about how you, and only you, can add value that is unique, something that no one else can replicate.

Anyone can talk about high level stuff; you know the overview kind of content that doesn't tell you anything new. Pretty obvious right? It should be. But, it's also something so many people do, and wonder why the masses don't come flocking to their door. News flash: it's because you are talking about the same thing people can find anywhere else on thousands of websites.

Yes, you need to cover the top level items, because as mentioned earlier in this book, without doing so, you aren't ensuring all of your audience have the same base level of knowledge. However, those articles aren't where the real value is (as important as they are).

Don't be anyone, be you. Tell your stories, share your experiences, add your personality, dive deeper, and be profound. One of the most effective ways I've seen of people going deeper into a topic is through questioning and contextualising.

This can be questioning conventional wisdom, questioning best practices, or, even better, questioning your own work and thoughts. Why is this good? Because questioning shows a deeper level of understanding, especially when you are challenging your own thoughts.

I'm a field hockey player, and I'm lucky enough to have played at a high level for a number of years (between knee operations), and one of the greatest things that helped me to improve my game play, was self-questioning. I could be honest with myself both good and bad. This reflective process gave me the realisation that I did a lot more good than bad, but that I could always make a few tweaks to constantly improve. Although, sometimes I was definitely too harsh on myself.

By questioning your own content and own ideas, you will be able to refine and improve them. Share those flaws, and how you identified and overcame them. That is raw, unadulterated content, that no one else can produce, and your audience will love you for it.

To provide value you have to go deeper. It's a bit like drilling for oil or mining for diamonds. It's not easy to get the rewards, but when you get down to that level you are going to roll around in your riches. The deeper you go, the more untapped value there is, and the bigger rewards you will have down the line.

One of the most important things I have learned building

my marketing career is to become T-shaped. I absolutely love this model, and think it's a great way of keeping me grounded.

I want you to imagine that the flat top of the T is surface level and the long vertical part is down in the ground (like a root). The top represents surface-level content, i.e. what things are and how they work. The vertical represents the depth and specificity of knowledge on a particular element i.e. your buzzword.

I believe that you need to understand the wider role of marketing and as many of its dimensions as possible in order to effectively teach people how a buzzword will affect their business. Without this wider view, knowledge and experience it is difficult for you to understand really how your given buzzword fits into a full picture.

It's about balance, but the deeper you go the more you are becoming a thought-leader, not a thought-copier. There are so many potential blogs you can read, and copy. That's great, but that doesn't really convey knowledge, expertise or authority.

You need to read around the subject, you need to digest other people's content and ideas, and question their validity, because that will help you form your own views.

It's also very much ok to ask your audience questions. You don't have to be the font of all knowledge in order to be an authority. Your audience will have thoughts, ideas and suggestions that can open your eyes, and give you perspectives that you hadn't considered. This will help make you a more rounded teacher, and give you more inspiration for content that contextualises the buzzword you are aligning yourself with.

Crowdsourcing ideas and opinions is a fantastic way to engage and invigorate your audience. The more they feel valued, the more they will talk, and the more they are likely to share. Especially when you are coining your own buzzword, you need to galvanise your audience and help them buy into it, and see the value in associating with it. People power.

The most important thing for you to do is remember the audience you are speaking to and connecting with.

- Chris Strub, I am here LLC

The Marketing Buzzword Podcast

FIFTEEN

HOW NOT TO BUILD A PERSONAL BRAND AROUND A BUZZWORD

"It ain't what you do, it's the way that you do it, that's what gets results"
– Fun Boy Three w/ Bananarama

Knowing how not to build a personal brand is as important to understand as knowing how to build one. There are so many errors, simple errors, that people make all too often. I know. I've been there. I've done it. I still make mistakes. That's OK, because I know I'm not perfect, but I'll always work to avoid as many as possible, and that's what I expect of you.

In this chapter I am going to break down some of the key things I see people doing, and (as mentioned in the last chapter) through crowdsourcing, what other authorities within marketing have learned over the time whilst they have been building their personal brands. This isn't going to be the complete guide to never making a mistake in your personal brand. There are thousands of blog posts out there for that. This chapter though, will break down, in detail, a number of things that could go wrong. It will also show you some examples of some amazing people who have built incredibly authoritative personal brands, how they have done it.

The most common, and easily avoided error made is thinking that just because it is good, and easy for you, it doesn't mean it's good and easy for your audience. And, as you should have noticed, one of the common themes through this book is that 'it's not about you'.

At this point I am going to point you to the man known as 'The Relentlessly Helpful Technical Copywriter', John Espirian. He is possibly the most helpful guy I know on social media. He writes content that is good for his audience, and easy for them to digest.

John Espirian Case Study

John Espirian is a technical copywriter. A writer who is doing things a bit differently. In this case study I wanted to share with you how John has built his personal brand and business brand over time, how John's commitment to being 'relentlessly helpful' has helped him to become a recognised authority.

So, where did it all start? John started his copywriting business back in 2009, following on from a career in software testing and quality assurance.

This career path meant that John had to do a lot of writing, in a simple, concise and clear manner. This is

because he needed to ensure that people maximised their time and didn't get frustrated with the process.

When John left that job, he knew that his biggest skill was the ability to explain 'how stuff works'. He knew he could write things that were easy to understand, in a way that wasn't salesy. That was the aim in 2009. And, what I love is that it's still the aim today.

Today, John is known as the 'Relentlessly Helpful Technical Copywriter'. This only came into existence from a chance answer to a question that Mark Schaefer asked him at an event called CMA Live in 2017 about what John wanted to be for his audience (you can actually find a post about this in an article John wrote for Mark Schaefer's blog herehttps://businessesgrow.-com/2018/10/25/branding-hook/. His answer: "To be relentlessly helpful".

As well as relatively recently positioning himself as being relentlessly helpful, John only started his blog in 2014 (some five years after starting the business).

The problem for John (as with many of us) back in 2014 is that he wasn't really sure what this content thing was, and how it would work. This meant that it didn't really take off.

As time passed, John started to get to grips with a little something called consistency, and the positive impact that could have on his website traffic. This growth in knowledge led him to join the CMA (Content

Marketing Academy) run by Chris Marr, where John got to learn not only off people like Chris, but also from experts such as Marcus Sheridan.

It was then towards the back-end of 2015 that all the pieces started coming together. He started to realise that creating helpful content was a better replacement for knocking on doors and traditional sales techniques.

John continued on this path of content creation, slowly building a bank of articles. He kept showing up, not just once every three months, but weekly because he knew that every quarter just wasn't enough, and he needed to be more consistent than that!

Moving into 2016 saw John keep pushing on, writing articles and bulking up his website as his base. He started to realise that his content was beginning to rank well on Google, and his footprint was growing.

This growth could not have been achieved had John not been posting regularly and consistently.

What I really love about John and his work is that he has stayed true to writing. He hasn't been drawn in by the shiny lights of new technologies and new mediums.

He understood that his service was writing, so it needed to be his main focus. In fact, he was even offered to take over a technical writing podcast, which he turned down in favour of doubling down on what he was good at.

As with everyone who has written and created a lot of content over their careers, John has definitely seen a shift in the quality and style of his work. Moving away from things like writing in third person to first. Also, by adding more personality and more humour. Even adding BitmoJohn gave John's content an extra 'fun factor'. John stopped falling into the trap of thinking 'this is how it is done', and instead focused on developing his own style.

The biggest adjustment he had to make aside from the content itself, was the channel in which John shared and promoted his content.

John used to do a lot of his content sharing via Twitter. But worked out that it wasn't really bringing in any value. For his personal brand it was OK, but not so in terms of convincing people to hire John. So, in 2017 John made a choice. The choice was to do a wholesale move over to LinkedIn.

After the switch, he found that not only was he getting more work, but he was also becoming more known. I can wholly attest to this. John shares an incredible amount of value on the platform, not only in his posts, but in the comments he leaves on others' posts. He really is being relentlessly helpful.

For this case study, I wanted to not only highlight how John has developed his personal brand and how he has become an authority in his space, but also how he is now going to maintain this over time.

What John hopes is that he will have created a big enough bank of content over the next few years that he won't have to keep creating the same volume of new stuff. Instead, he will begin going deeper, and adding more details.

In essence, making each piece even more epic! Right now, John is continuing to be helpful, and growing his influence. He is now at the stage where he is considering taking his writing to the next level with a book too.

I'm really excited to see what's next for John, and follow his progress. I highly recommend that you do too!

John has avoided that all too common trap of not adding value to his audience. His personal brand and his reputation has soared because of it, and ultimately he's also completely booked up with work. Win-win.

Another error that often appears when people embark on their personal branding journey is a lack of planning and structure. This all too often comes from not having a 'why' and a 'where' (why are you building a personal brand, and where do you want it to take you).

I'm one of the lucky ones. From about 16 or so I had a pretty good idea of what I wanted, and where I wanted to go. My goal was (and still is) to be the CMO (Chief Marketing Officer) of a FTSE 250 by the time I am 30. At the time of writing this is 2018/19, I am 26, that gives me about three and a half years.

Everything I have done to this point, am now doing

(including writing this book), and everything I will do up to the age of 30 will be to help me get to my goal. That is my why.

Because I have a why, I have something to aim for. This end-point means I can plan and have a structure. This structure means I can consistently create valuable content for my audience, and without making anything I produce about me, I can still get some personal value. Ultimately, structure and planning helps to create consistency. And, as I've already mentioned, consistency is core.

At this point I want to introduce you to another person I admire, who is helping people and brands to avoid this. Sonja Jefferson is a woman who I only met about 6 months prior to writing this book, but I was instantly blown away with her approach to creating 'valuable content'.

Sonja Jefferson Case Study

Sonja Jefferson is the founder of Valuable Content (https://www.valuablecontent.co.uk), a specialist marketing agency in the UK. She is also the author of the book; *Valuable Content Marketing – how to make content the key to your business success.* As is probably pretty obvious already, Sonja has been building both a personal brand, and a business brand around the term; valuable content.

This career focus on valuable content stemmed from a lightbulb moment. Sonja had worked in professional sales for a decade and came to the realisation that sharing information that was genuinely valuable, interesting and helpful for your clients was the very best way to get them to know, like, trust and remember you – a great way to build great client relationships and to win the business you need.

This was the mid-1990s and 'content' wasn't really a thing at the time. Sonja read widely and came across the work of David Meerman Scott and his amazing book; *The New Rules of Marketing and PR*[1]. David talked about the power of helping over selling and Sonja's valuable content business development methodology was ignited.

Sonja then began creating sales and marketing content for clients that was actually helpful, living up to the principles she wanted to share with businesses. Her interest is to create stories, and narratives that helped people to understand, and get value from the businesses they interact with.

This was all great but Sonja needed to prove the power of the valuable content approach. She began adding new elements to her marketing.

It started with the Valuable Content Awards. These were created to reward success and to share stories and examples of what was possible in if you consistently created helpful, inspiring content for your audience. This developed into regular meet ups and talks and a book (Valuable Content Marketing) to share the guiding principles of valuable content.

The more that Sonja talked and presented her ideas

around valuable content, the more her reputation grew (I know I can vouch for that having seen her speak at least twice at the time of writing this) and continues to grow. She's now very much seen as an authority in the content space.

The problem with being seen as an authority on a topic is maintaining it. This is something that Sonja has to deal with, as you will too. And, if you're like Sonja, you really won't like letting people down.

She avoids this risk by setting a pattern to her marketing and communication. She sets systems for things like her email newsletters. This means that she can stay front of mind, she can have a time and place in people's weeks where they know she will be.

It's not just about the systems though. It's also about the research. Sonja is constantly looking at new angles, new examples and new ideas. She uses surveys and interviews to understand and stay relevant; to keep her finger on the pulse.

As well as adding new elements to her business and personal brand over time, she's also pivoted. Not just for her audience, but also for herself. To keep herself motivated and excited.

As mentioned earlier, it started off with the blogs, then the advisory service, next the book and the speaking. Sonja and her agency then began the training element, where they focussed on upskilling marketers and businesses with the knowledge they need to put together their own valuable content.

What Sonja is now finding, is what many business owners and business leaders find; that consistent change and flex is needed. This change will mean that Sonja will be able to stay relevant, stay excited and remain committed to providing value to her audience.

What I love about this is that Sonja hasn't feared the change, but she's embracing it. She has worked with coaches over the years to help her remain clear and focused. This enables her to continue her mission of helping people and businesses to create truly valuable content, pulling the right people towards them and winning great business so they thrive.

Make sure you take a look at Sonja's Valuable Content website, it's jam-packed full of goodness: https://www.valuablecontent.co.uk

I love Sonja's approach. It's frankly refreshing, and really gets people thinking about the direction they are heading with their content.

That being said, extensive planning isn't for everyone, and not everyone has to extensively plan. Your plan could be loose, and without complete detailing. However, there always must be a point, and a reason for what you are doing. As Simon Sinek wrote 'start with why'.[2]

When you are building your personal brand, be personal. An error that far too many make is to not be themselves. It can be like the camera, the microphone or the keyword is a black hole, sucking people's fun and personalities. This leads to bland content. Maybe your audience wants bland content? I'd hedge my bets and say that they don't though!

Bland content is not inspiring, and not engaging. If you are finding that your chosen medium is draining on your personality, and you are finding your own content boring, you need to change things up (remember that if you aren't enjoying or want to watch your own content, then why would your audience?).

What you will find is that mediums like video can be draining. You have to put in huge amounts of energy into your videos in order to actually look like you have a personality. Also with mediums like podcasting where you can only stimulate people's audio senses, you have to talk, in a way that holds attention, and captures the imagination.

It's not always easy, but if you use the rule of thumb 'would I listen to/watch that myself?' then you will be in a far better position than many people who are also looking to build their personal brands. Put yourself in the shoes of your audience, or even better, actually ask them. Make sure that your medium is right, and your personality fits. Do that and you will have avoided a common pitfall many fail to see.

The final error that I want to address in detail is the length of time it takes to get to the point. It's imperative that you remember that people are watching your videos, reading your blogs or listening to your podcast for a reason. The reasons can differ, but you have to give them some value early on, so they know to keep consuming the content to get even more of what they crave.

I'm not going to quote that 9-second goldfish attention span[3] nonsense, because frankly it's been proven false, even though people still love to quote it in their talks.

What is true though, is that if your content doesn't capture and hold people's attentions they will turn off. The more valuable, the funnier, the better quality the content, the more likely you are to win their attention, for longer.

One of the most difficult mediums to get this right with is live streaming. If you wait a few minutes after you go live in order to get more people to join the video before you deliver value, you have wasted the people's time who got there earlier, but if you start early with the value there is a risk that most people won't have yet joined the live stream, and they could miss some essential grounding information.

There is not a set answer for this, but something you should consider is that live videos will save, which means people will be able to watch anything that they have missed. Consider focussing on the audience that are with you in the here and now. Get straight to the point, hold their attention and they will come back to you in the future.

Your personal brand is yours, and yours alone. The mistakes are yours to bear too, but so are the fruits of your work. Learn from the mistakes of others, implement the ideas presented in this book, and both your audience and authority will grow.

The hardest part of personal branding is keeping consistent with that initial impression.

- Brian Fanzo, isocialfanz

The Marketing Buzzword Podcast

SIXTEEN

HOW AND WHY YOU MAY NEED TO PIVOT

"You change your business plan to anticipate and adapt to changes in the marketplace."
- Jon Feltheimer

Pivoting is arguably one of the most important parts of sustaining an effective personal brand over time. Pivoting is not something to be ashamed of, nor is it a negative. Instead it should be viewed as an incredible positive, in the sense that you are adapting to changes in the environment. I'm pretty sure everyone can agree too that the world is changing. Fast. This pace of change is mirrored by the creation and evolution of buzzwords. The more changes, the more buzzwords.

The negative perception of pivoting comes from the people who appear to constantly change where their focus is. One week they are an expert on cryptocurrency, the next they are a Facebook Ads specialist, and the week after a Financial Services Technical Content Writer.

It's that type of constant pivoting that you must avoid. Because it is inconsistent. You must remember consistency is at the core of what you do, and everything else is built out from it. This lack of consistency is also viewed as untrustworthy, and your knowledge perceived as limited. That is because it is impossible to build trust and authority over a matter of weeks, even a few months. It takes years.

Change is good though, and it is absolutely OK (if not even encouraged) to change your focus. If you don't stay mobile and pivot, then there is a chance you will get left behind. That is because as I've pointed out, there will always be new buzzwords, new technologies, and new innovations.

There are some great examples of people who have built their personal brands on a platform or around a buzzword, and have had to pivot, either by choice, or because of changes in the market.

One of my favourite examples is that of Brian Fanzo. I've been following him for years. And, in all honesty, at first I wasn't a fan. It took time, but his consistency, authenticity and quality of content over time converted me.

Today I listen to Brian's FOMO Fanz podcast (https://www.isocialfanz.com/fomofanz/) and follow him on pretty much all the social media platforms that I use. He first built his audience in one place, pivoted, took many of those existing fans with him, and added new ones on top. An amazing feat of personal branding, and a model that can and will work for you.

If you are thinking about pivoting, or may be likely to pivot at some time in the future, then you need to communicate that clearly. You need to tell your audience why, and seek to reduce the confusion. People don't panic or fear what is already a part of the plan. In addition, by being clear with your audience, you are further creating an environment of openness and transparency.

People fear abrupt change, without warning. To quote The Joker in Christopher Nolan's The Dark Knight; "You know what I noticed? Nobody panics when things go according to plan. Even when the plan is horrifying. If tomorrow I told the press that, like, a gang-banger would get shot, or a truckload of soldiers will be blown up, nobody panics. Because it's all part of the plan". I love this quote. The person it's from may have a questionable moral compass, but the sentiment is right.

When you are looking to pivot you should communicate why, and share the potential benefits they will see from this pivot. Do this and they are likely to stick with you, because they already like, know and trust you. Think back to the earlier case study with Dan Gingiss, that's what he did, and his personal brand has continued to go from strength to strength since.

At this point, it's worth clarifying that pivoting doesn't always mean a full change of direction. It doesn't have to mean a full 90 degree turn, it can be subtler. Smaller changes are a lot easier to manage, as they potentially require less communication and are less likely to have a significant short-term impact on your audience, but still allow you to remain at the forefront of your industry and the market. However, there are still risks.

One of which is that by subtly changing, you lose your core audience almost without knowing it, as you haven't clearly communicated your change to them, and they have felt neglected. At least with a hard turn, and clear direction, you can be very clear about your direction, and your audience will choose to follow you or not, instead of being left to feel neglected.

Often people will resist pivoting until they are forced to do so for fear of losing their existing audience. I can understand that. You've worked hard to build your audience, you've invested countless hours and significant sums of money in some cases. Your audience is your baby, and you don't want to lose it.

However, without pivoting, no matter the size or depth of your investment, you could be limiting yourself and your potential (I say 'could', because it depends on the buzzword and platform in question and environmental factors that are in-play). You can't ignore changes in the market, and yes, if you do pivot there is a chance you will lose some of your audience. But, if you are moving to a platform with a new potential audience, or transitioning to a growth buzzword, then you will soon win back more customers and exceed your existing audience size (do remember though that size isn't everything, it is quality that matters).

Change isn't always your choice. Sometimes it is forced upon you. What are you going to do then? Fold like a deck of cards? Or find a new angle?

Today's business and marketing world is changing rapidly, this means that more so than ever before, some previously advanced technologies and tactics are heading the way of the Dodo. How many people are now growing businesses around the topic of direct mail marketing? Not many. The audience isn't there anymore. They've moved off, and the people that were once experts in that field have since transitioned away. There were people who used to talk about the power of technologies and platforms Blab, Google+, Myspace, Meerkat and Vine.

These were all up and coming social media and marketing platforms, but have since disappeared, or become integrated within bigger platforms. Influencer, experts and users have all had to adapt and move on. These are just some examples of where things change, and you as an expert have to adapt with the times.

You need to consider your personal brand like a business. Would you change your product offering by choice without telling your customers? No. At least I hope not, especially if your product offering is limited (same as the number of areas of business that you have deep knowledge on). Even if the choice is forced upon you, you would tell them, right? The answer is yes.

If you do lose some of your audience that's OK. That's part of transitioning. You have to keep your mind focused on the medium- and long-term and not let the fear of the unknown hold you back. Because overall you are going to end up in a much more positive position. Embrace the change.

The key to online courses is the transformation. People are purchasing online courses because it's a specific shortcut. Yeah, you could go to YouTube, but it is time-consuming and not necessarily a whole journey or step-by-step guide. It's about taking you from one state to another.

- Rob Balasabas, Thinkific

The Marketing Buzzword Podcast

SEVENTEEN

BECOMING THE AUTHORITY THAT YOUR INDUSTRY NEEDS

"Our job is obvious: We need to get out of the way, shine a light, and empower a new generation to teach itself and to go further and faster than any generation ever has."
— Seth Godin

In wrapping up this part of the book I wanted to be really straight with you about some of the non-negotiables, and some of the areas which you fill find particularly difficult to navigate. Because becoming an authority isn't easy. Nor is it a quick process. It is instead a long road, and there are no overnight successes (and if you think there are, they were actually probably years in the making).

It will take time, and you cannot skip straight to the end. You may be able to speed up parts of the process, but you cannot go straight for the summit without first tackling the mountain beneath it.

Keeping with the climbing a mountain analogy; you do not

climb a mountain by sprinting up it, stopping, sprinting, stopping and continuing that cycle, over and over. For some it may be possible, but that's not the most efficient, and in fact, it would actually take longer.

Putting this back in the context of trying to become an authority. You need to be consistent. This consistency is at the core of your attempts to build an authority. This means consistently producing high value content, designed for your target audience / customer.

Consistency is your commitment to your audience. If you say you are going to do something, then your audience expect it. This includes committing to a weekly podcast, a daily video or a bi-weekly blog post. Delivering on this commitment is your opportunity to build trust. If you let your audience down, and you are severely damaging the faith and trust they are putting in you, that is no way to become a marketing authority.

If you miss a tweet or a Facebook post, your reputation isn't going to take an instant nose dive. It all depends on your commitment. The more you commit, the more you have to gain, but you also have more to lose.

Getting the balance right isn't easy. You need to think long-term, but make short-term moves – like the game of chess we talked about earlier. You need to assess where you are going, and why. From there you will be able to work backwards. Always remembering that it's not about you, it's never about you, and should never be about you. That's the key to building a personal brand around a buzzword.

Spend time having conversations, and getting to know people because you know at the end of the day people are going to buy from you if they know, like and trust you. The way that happens is through conversation.

- Madalyn Sklar, #TwitterSmarter

The Marketing Buzzword Podcast

PART THREE
BUZZWORDS FOR BUSINESS

Now that we've explored the opportunities and considerations required to build a personal brand, we now need to explore how businesses and business brands can also leverage the opportunities presented by buzzwords. After all, according to the UK's Office of National Statistics, in 2018, 27.44 million people (84.7% of all people in work) are employed by a business or corporation[1]. This means that the vast majority of the population are employed by someone else. This is why it's not only important to understand how to build a personal brand around a buzzword, but how to build it within an existing brand.

You will more than likely find a number of similarities between this part of the book and part two. However, the context is different and the practical applications also differ. The key theme in this section is the binding together of a company and a business brand with a buzzword. It will feature case studies from brands who are doing this right now, and others that have successfully done it in the past.

If you are easy to do business with. If it's no hassle and there is a great system. People will come back. Why? Because it's just so darn convenient.

- *Shep Hyken, Hyken*

The Marketing Buzzword Podcast

EIGHTEEN

USING A BUZZWORD AS A COMMON THREAD

"When you're surrounded by people who share a passionate commitment around a common purpose, anything is possible."

- Howard Schultz, Starbucks

Your business (either the one you own, or one you work for) will more than likely have a mission statement, or strategic set of goals. But are these statements something that your employees, or you as an employee can really buy into? Are these elements something you can write helpful content around? Is that goal something that will help deliver value to your customers? Maybe, but probably not. Most mission statements are written by some top level exec with some grand idea, but in reality, it means nothing to the everyday boots on the ground or for your customers.

I'm not saying that those company goals are redundant or not important, because that isn't true. They have a brilliant purpose. However, they aren't really designed for the customers' benefit.

Therefore, I propose that on top of your existing goals or mission statement you look to bring in a buzzword or phrase that becomes your common thread. Something that everyone from top down, or bottom up can invest in.

COMMON THREAD DEFINITION: AN IDEA OR THEME THAT IS CONSISTENTLY PRESENT IN SEVERAL DIFFERENT AREAS OR THINGS. IT HELPS TO LINK AND BIND ALL OF AREAS OR THINGS TOGETHER.[1]

Some of you may have heard the following quote before 'all roads lead to Rome'. This is the principle that I am looking for you to implement in your businesses. This quote means that all paths or activities lead to the centre of things (your given buzzword). And, to give you some historical background around the quote; it was literally true in the days of the Roman Empire, one of the world's largest empires, when all the empire's roads radiated out from, and led to the capital city, Rome. What this quote doesn't say though is that the Romans actually invented roads. So, naturally they carved out the roads from their point of origin.

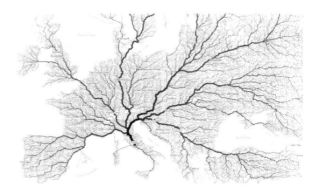

http://www.openculture.com/2018/05/an-
interactive-map-shows-just-how-many-roads-
actually-lead-to-rome.html

In the case of the Roman Empire and your business, you should have something to radiate out from and create paths for people to follow back to the original source.

As an example, we will use the buzzword 'Social Selling'. Social selling is your common thread, now all the roads off it will be answering specific questions, solving problems, offering guidance and advice. These paths will reach out into the world, and give potential customers a chance to reach you. The more and better quality of your paths, the more likely they are to find their way to your business.

Much like how you can build a personal brand around an existing buzzword (as we've just discussed), you can also build out from a term you have coined. You can use this coined term, and use your home base (most likely your website) to build your roads out from. The principle is the same as the 'social selling' idea we just looked at, but the roads aren't already built (people aren't already searching for your term). You have to outreach and graft to build these roads yourself with content related to your given term. It's a lot of effort, but much like building a personal brand, the benefits of coining your own term are yours, you have the first-mover advantage.

It is important to remember, that as discussed earlier in the book, the more common a buzzword, the more competition there will be. This, metaphorically speaking, will mean more roads, and more potential directions people can go. Therefore, it is extremely important you maintain your existing roads (by updating your content), and continue to lay new roads so that people can keep finding their way to you (by creating new content).

To effectively do this, and potentially reach a much wider pool of customers than you currently have, you should consider using your employees and their personal brands. By encouraging them to do this you are creating mini hubs of relevant content (using the common thread discussed previously), which will amplify your messages and help your 'road network' to outstretch further.

This technique works brilliantly. Firstly, because it allows your marketing messages and branding to be shared further than the brand could do so alone. Secondly, it allows for the individuals to use their own experiences, ideas and personality to create different types and styles of content, but all remaining in keeping with the company's common thread.

By using this common thread method, you have to trust your employees with their personal brands and work with them to ensure that they can use their own voices, and unique styles. You need to constantly and consistently work with them to keep this going. This is to ensure that both the individual and the business are singing from the same hymn sheet, because it can be really bad for the business if the goals aren't aligned.

In the next chapter, I will go into a lot more detail about how to properly align each individual's personal brand with your company's brand using a buzzword. But, one of the key ideas I want to really hammer home is that the central theme will help to create a culture of learning and improvement within your organisation, and encourage increased intrapreneurship (the idea of employees innovating and creating concepts and ideas within the business itself).

People are one of your brand's biggest assets, so the ability to leverage their potential is of huge significance. When they feel empowered to have a creative licence to create content in a way that best suits them, and it is totally aligned with the company's common thread, you are going to increase innovation. This innovation will help your company to stand out. This means no more stale, bland, vanilla content. No more boringness.

There is a saying that competition breeds improvement. This is not only the case between businesses, but also within organisations and departments such as the marketing team. As Head of Marketing at Talkative (https://talkative.uk), this is what I am trying to do with my team.

We have a game called 'BackLink to the Future' (I know, great name). For this game, everyone is tasked with obtaining high quality, relevant backlinks to our website. The higher the domain authority of a website, and the more relevant it is, the more points you get. Over the period of a month the person with the most points wins. Over time I've had to slightly adapt this game and bring in handicaps in order to keep the starting points as level as possible to ensure there is an equal enough opportunity for all to win.

Backlink to the future

Domain Authority	Points per "follow" backlink
0-29	1
30-49	2
50-59	4
60-69	6
70-79	8
80-89	9
90-100	10 & bottle of bubbly

Rules

- Follow backlinks only.
- The winner is the person with the most backlinks.
- In the case of a draw (equal number of points), the winner if the person with the highest number of unique domains. If there is still a tie, the winner will be the person with the biggest number of total links in that month.
- To have a backlink attributed, it must be picked up in either Moz or Ahrefs.
- Only backlinks accrued between the first day, and the last day of the month according to Moz or Ahrefs will be counted for that month.
- If an individual wins two months in a row, they shall receive a handicap to level the playing field.

I've found this game to be a brilliant source of motivation, innovation and self-improvement for the team as a whole, and the individuals within it. It is also all completely aligned with the goals and common thread of the business (in the corporate world, people may define this as 'strategic alignment').

STRATEGIC ALIGNMENT DEFINITION: THE PROCESS OF BRINGING THE ACTIONS OF AN ORGANISATION'S BUSINESS DIVISIONS AND STAFF MEMBERS IN-LINE WITH THE ORGANISATION'S PLANNED OBJECTIVES. THE ABILITY OF MOST BUSINESSES TO ACHIEVE THEIR STRATEGIC GOALS WILL BENEFIT FROM PERFORMING A COMPREHENSIVE STRATEGIC ALIGNMENT TO HELP ASSURE THAT ITS DIVISIONS AND EMPLOYEES ARE JOINTLY WORKING TOWARD THE COMPANY'S STATED GOALS.[2]

Common goals, common terminology, common culture. This is part of how you can use a buzzword to build a business brand. I found an amazing example of this with a company called Yext (https://www.yext.co.uk). They've coined the buzzword Digital Knowledge Management (DKM), and are now using that as a term around which they can become synonymous with.

Yext Case Study

Yext are a brilliant company that I have previously featured on my podcast. The reason; they have coined their own term that they are now using to help build their brand.

To give you some context, and some idea of what they do, here is an extract from their website: "Yext's mission is to give companies control over their brand experiences across the digital universe of maps, apps, search engines, voice assistants, and other intelligent services that drive consumer discovery, decision, and action." In essence, they have a lot of experience in search, and digital data management (all the bits of information about you and your company online).

So, naturally I was curious as to how this term they been using, "digital knowledge management" (DKM) came about. The answer was as simple as you could probably imagine. External of Yext, the phrase likely already existed, but internally, the idea took root on its own. It came from people discussing ideas, where someone just said it, and asked; "what do you think?" This was then tested internally at first in order to gauge the opinions of the people who would be using the term on a daily basis.

Once they saw that the term resonated internally, it was now time to externalise it. This was the make or break moment and thankfully for Yext, it went well. In fact, so well that people began latching onto and talking about the term, even creating jobs under the title of "Digital Knowledge Manager".

What Yext also saw from this externalisation were benefits in the form of search and the customer journey. From the search perspective, as the momentum started to build, and people were looking at what the term meant, Yext were ranking in the search results. In addition, the customer journey improved too as it allowed Yext to be able to better distribute information to the right people, at the right stage of the buying journey.

By using this term "Digital Knowledge Management", Yext have been able to pull many areas of their business together. Before using this term, everyone knew what the products and solutions were but there wasn't a thing that helped bring them all together into one package. It helped solve a problem.

When I was building out this case study on Yext, I spoke to Duane Forrester, their VP of Industry Insights, who was the former Head of Bing Webmaster Tools about his thoughts on the term, and why it was important. His response was brilliant.

Firstly, he made the point that his previous job made him very aware of how things were changing, and how search was evolving. He then went on to talk about how people are beginning not to search, instead, through devices like Alexa people are getting information direct from source. This means that companies, now more than ever, have to get their data management right. That's the niche that Yext fills. They are partnering with brands and services like Alexa to get this digital knowledge right. The ultimate goal being perfect data everywhere.

What's been great to see since Yext started using this term is that other people are genuinely starting to use it. And, as mentioned right at the start of this case study, there are now jobs being advertised for "Digital Knowledge Managers".

Yext, are now able to have better conversations with

their customers, and more relevant conversations. DKM has enabled Yext to stay ahead of their competitors and be at the forefront of conversations within their industry. This is the power of coining your own term, as discussed all the way back in chapter nine.

When I asked Yext for this case study, I was not only intrigued to find out about how they are building authority around this term, but also their 'why'.

Their 'why' started with the understanding that they needed to begin expanding from just local listings. They realised that everything is a digital asset, and that businesses need to get all of their online data in order.

Yext also believe that this is the beginning of a new phase in digital era (I'm definitely inclined to agree). The way that data is used and searched for is changing, and consumers are driving that change vociferously.

The term Digital Knowledge Management isn't just a buzzword for Yext, it's a way of thinking, and philosophy that all their employees can buy into. That's why it's successful, and that's why it will continue to be so. I for one, am definitely looking forward to seeing what the future holds for Yext and DKM.

Make sure you take a look at Yext's website to do a deep-dive into DKM: https://www.yext.com

Yext are building a network of digital knowledge management content, reaching out from their website. They are building their own road network, and all the traffic that gets onto those roads finds its way to Yext's website. That's the power of coining your own term.

When you're thinking about your business, and how you run it, you don't have to conform to the way that's always been done. You also don't have to do it the way that your competition run their business or set up their business model.

- Chris Marr, Content Marketing Academy

The Marketing Buzzword Podcast

NINETEEN

USING PERSONAL BRANDS WITHIN EXISTING BUSINESS BRANDS

"All of us need to understand the importance of branding. We are CEOs of our own companies: Me Inc. To be in business today, our most important job is to be head marketer for the brand called You."

– Tom Peters in Fast Company

O K, personal branding. It's been mentioned a lot already in this book. But, this chapter will not be like part two. Instead of looking through the lens of the individual, we are going to look through the eyes of a business.

As mentioned at the beginning of part three of this book, a business's employees are probably their biggest asset (and one of the biggest costs). As a business brand you have a single voice. When you create content that's purely attributed to the organisation, and not the individuals, you are limiting your reach. This is because as powerful as your brand's single voice may well be, it cannot be compared to the power that a number of small voices can have. When working harmoniously, the co-ordinated efforts of lots of small voices, can cause a tirade of noise.

A general life lesson: never ignore the little guy, you never know how much real power they can wield, for good or bad.

I look at the power of personal brands as like having little speakers dotted around a huge room, and the main business brand being the big speakers at the end. You can have those speakers at the end of the room blasting as loud as you can, but by the time the sound gets to the back of the room it could be pretty quiet, distorted or just unclear. By adding in smaller (less powerful) speakers around the room, you are able to clearly amplify the same content to everyone in the room (the target audience).

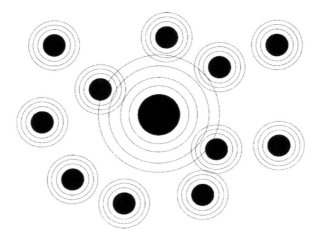

To allow all these small voices to build their personal brands and speak up requires trust, sometimes a lot of it. This is where large numbers of employers get nervous about allowing their employees to build their personal brands let alone even talking about the company on social media.

Businesses are still stuck in the old way of thinking that they don't want their employees to talk about the business online. They are still scared to give away that control. They see it as a huge risk. They perceive that the individuals trying to build a personal brand are doing it so that they can look for a new job or ask for ludicrously high pay rises. This may be the case for the minority but for most individuals it isn't the case.

I would be 100% lying to you if I said that the risk wasn't there, and that there was an existing method for completely nullifying it. However, that simply isn't the case. You can manage it, and by actually being positive and progressive, it's a huge positive.

You as a business can spend time with your employees, work out their motives, objectives and desires, and find a way to align those thoughts with the goals of your business.

Trust has to come from both parties. You cannot demand trust without giving anything in return and vice versa. It also requires clear, concise, and open communication from both parties. Both should be demanding of the other to keep in constant contact. The more open you are, as a business and a marketing authority, the easier it is for trust to build.

It is of vital importance that you are looking to work closely with your employees and seeking to empower them to create content that aligns their ideas with those of the business. Leaders and businesses that see themselves as being empowering, by definition, attempt to give power back to their employees by providing them with what is variously referred to as autonomy, discretion, control, or decision latitude.

In response to the actions of an empowering leader of business, employees can be expected to feel more motivated and to be more likely to have enhanced role-related feelings of contribution, control, competence, connection, value and meaning. This will in turn reduce an employees' propensity to want to change jobs, as they are currently being fulfilled by their existing one.

If your employees buy-into the common thread running through your business (your buzzword), and you give them the latitude to be able to create relevant, and highly authoritative content on the subject you will be rewarded.

Getting the blend right isn't easy. But, you are more likely to get it right by engaging with them, and having dialogue on a consistent basis. Regular dialogue is not only designed to keep you both on the same page (making sure that the content remains on brand), it is also there to help encourage and motivate.

Intrapreneurship is also something that I've previously briefly covered in this book, but I now want to explore in more detail. And I will do so by starting with a definition.

Intrapreneurship definition: Intrapreneurship is acting like an entrepreneur within a larger organisation. Intrapreneurs are usually highly self-motivated, proactive and action-oriented people who are comfortable with taking the initiative, even within the boundaries of an organisation, in pursuit of an innovative product or service.[1]

The link between intrapreneurship and buzzwords is that intrapreneurship helps you and/or your business or organisation to be more creative, and more innovative than your competitors. It will allow you to not simply create content around your given buzzword, but to truly get ahead and stay ahead of your competitors.

What gaps are there in your market? Can you empower your employees to become influencers from within your business? Can they host a podcast? Video show? Vlog? Are they an amateur cartoonist? Have they got loads to say, that would work well for micro-blogging? Are they a creative content writer who can create powerful narratives?

Maybe you know the answers to some of the above questions. Maybe you don't. Either way you need to give your employees, your colleagues and anyone in the organisation the opportunity to contribute, have their voice heard and feel valued, as long as it aligns with your business' core values and guidelines.

Every single person in your organisation will have their own unique experiences, skills, ideas and personalities. In order to harness those, you need to build a culture of 'it's absolutely ok to create the content you want, as long as it's within brand guidelines'. This also shouldn't be limited to just the marketing department. The dev team, the sales team, the customer service team, they all have roles to play in this.

It is so much more than a few blog posts or a couple of videos. By aligning your company branding efforts with your employees' personal branding efforts, you can create a mutually beneficial environment where everyone wins. It's not about one department going it alone, or others thinking, 'we're not marketing' so they shouldn't create content. It's a team effort.

This comes from the top down, not bottom up. A fish rots from the head down, but equally with the right management and leadership the organisation below can flourish.

I've found that a really effective way in which to begin developing this culture of building, developing and nurturing employees' personal brands, is to create 'internal influencers'. These are individuals within your business who are going to help drive forward your agenda for increasing the number of employees with growing personal brands, that are aligned with the agreed upon common thread (buzzword).

These individuals do not have to be at a certain level within the organisation such as management level, junior level, or even within a specific department. They just have to be individuals who also buy into the company's common thread and can have an impact on their peers.

You would need to identify and recruit these internal influencers in a similar way as you would an external influencer. You would also need to train and educate them as to the benefits of building a personal brand, and how those personal brands can remain very much aligned with the company's common thread and ideals.

By using this tactic of internal influencers you are able to build a culture throughout all levels of the business. You are also able to build authority across a range of individuals, that will help cushion the impact of any leaving the company, and will give more flexibility in terms of teaching new members of staff. This in turn will be supporting those already in the business to build their own authority and share their ideas.

As valuable as having your own tribe, your own niche, and people, it's also important to have an open mind and embrace the power of collaboration. That's how we make the most powerful connections.

- Jen Cole, DepICT Media

The Marketing Buzzword Podcast

TWENTY

THE SEO POWER OF USING A BUZZWORD

"The only thing to do with good advice is to pass it on. It is never of any use to oneself."
- Oscar Wilde

SEO (Search Engine Optimisation) might be a bit of a buzzword of the past; but it is very much alive. Yes, SEO ISN'T DEAD. As discussed very early in this book, SEO is one of those buzzwords that has become part of everyday vocabulary and is still constantly adapting and changing as the environment, algorithms and technology does around it.

In order for you to improve your search engine rankings you have to consider a number of factors. This includes keywords, page load speed, content depth and quality, backlinks and site structure.

For this chapter we are going to focus on two key areas: keywords, and content depth and quality.

Starting with keywords. There are two types: long-tail and short-tail. A buzzword by itself will more than likely be regarded as a short-tail keyword. This is a broad term which isn't a direct question, and may not evoke a specific response. Some examples of which would be 'Social Selling' or 'User Generated Content'.

SHORT-TAIL KEYWORDS: THESE ARE KEYWORD TERMS, ONE TO TWO WORDS IN LENGTH. THESE ARE BROAD MATCH TERMS, WHICH ARE USUALLY GENERAL, AND HAVE BOTH HIGH LEVELS OF COMPETITION AS WELL AS LARGE SEARCH VOLUMES.

LONG-TAIL KEYWORDS: GENERALLY REFERRED TO AS KEYWORD PHRASES, OVER 3 WORDS IN LENGTH. THEY ARE AIMED AT GETTING SPECIFIC RESPONSES, NOT BROAD RESULTS. THEY ARE GENERALLY LESS COMPETITIVE THAN BROADER TERMS, BUT ALSO HAVE LESS SEARCH VOLUME.

These are common terms that you will rank for over time if you have a back catalogue of high quality and highly relevant content related to the term. They are though, highly competitive for the most part (unless you've coined your own term), and you may find it hard to rank in the top ten search results. If though, you are able to rank in the top 10, you are likely to begin obtaining good search traffic (your organic results in Google Analytics).

However, ranking for these short-tail keywords is time consuming. In order to rank quicker, and for more specialised words, you will need to look at long-tail variations for your buzzword. This will require answering questions, digging deeper and being a lot more specific. Some examples of this might be: 'How do online reviews impact the online sales process' or 'How to use machine learning and artificial intelligence for ecommerce businesses'.

By using a buzzword as your central pillar you are able to create a wealth of long-tail-based content. Which, in turn, will have an extremely positive impact on your short-tail rankings. What's more, by creating content that is valuable and insightful for your customers and audience, you will already be putting yourself in a good position to rank for long-tail keywords. That is because you are already answering their questions. These are questions that they will be asking of search engines.

You can use a couple of different methods for discovering these exact questions. Initially by talking directly with your audience, or alternatively through the use of online tools such as Moz (https://moz.com), Ahrefs (https://ahrefs.com) or SEMRush (https://www.semrush.com).

These tools I've mentioned are the ones I use daily. They will be able to give you exact insights and data into which questions are being asked most often, which are getting the most traffic, and which have the highest or lowest levels of competition.

Whether you decide to go with your gut or the data, it is important that you are looking to answer questions asked by both your prospective and current customers. If you do this in a coherent, detailed and to-the-point manner, you will be able to not only rank highly, but become featured in Google's highly coveted 'knowledge boxes'. These are given pride of place at the top of search results, which is where you ultimately want to be. This has benefits not only in terms of visibility, but also in terms of visual appeal (they are formatted differently from the rest of Google's search results). This elevated status is an opportunity to again put your brand front and centre of a buzzword, so that you can become synonymous with it.

One of the best examples of this is Hubspot (https://www.hubspot.com). They are known for coining the term 'inbound marketing'. They dominate the search engines for searches of inbound marketing. They have become synonymous. They have consistently been creating quality content that solves problems over time (a bit of a theme throughout the book, right?).

This didn't just happen overnight though. It was and still is a long-term strategy. And they had to do it without an existing audience in place for the buzzword. However, they are now reaping the rewards, in part because the word they based their business around has since become part of everyday vocabulary and the search volume for the term increased massively.

This is a technique that you too can use for your business. Not necessarily to the same scale as Hubspot, but the guiding principle is the same. Especially if you are to look at coining your own term as discussed at the beginning of part two.

In order to make your SEO efforts worthwhile, and to dominate the sphere over time, you have to constantly monitor your efforts, and make adjustments when needed. There is absolutely no point creating content and leaving it because someone else will write something newer and better. It sounds harsh, but it is true. You cannot rest on your laurels.

Things never stand still in SEO, and search engine rankings are ever fluctuating. So too are your audience's / customers' questions, desires and search terms. If you want to stay relevant, and at the top of the rankings, you need to not only be creating new and unique content, but also updating and upgrading old content so that it maintains its accuracy and usefulness.

SEO is not dead, it's also not dying. Even if you are reading this book one, two or three years after it was published, I'm willing to bet that SEO still won't be dead. It may be different (perhaps because of voice searching), but it definitely won't be dead.

Therefore, it is still one of the most important ways to get found online and build authority. If you can improve your standings and reach page one for some of your core keywords you will be putting yourself in an incredibly powerful position to become an authority, without having to spend huge amounts of money.

Ask yourself: Why am I doing this? People try and run competitions on social media for vanity metrics. These vanity metrics won't necessarily translate to the outcome you want. You will just get people signing up to get more free stuff.

- Desiree Martinez, All-In-One Social Media

The Marketing Buzzword Podcast

TWENTY-ONE

BECOME THE WIKI OF YOUR BUZZWORD

"Knowledge is power. Information is liberating. Education is the premise of progress, in every society, in every family."

- Kofi Annan

Wikipedia (https://www.wikipedia.org) is arguably one of the most powerful and notable websites in the entire world. Even though it can be updated and changed by anyone, it is still one of the most trusted sources of information because of all the references it uses.

Wikipedia is a font of knowledge, for all things. However, there are also specific variations for popular and / or complex things (often which are popular with society, or important to it) which contain lots of details and subtleties. Some examples include:

- Star Wars (https://starwars.fandom.com/ wiki/Main_Page)

- Lord of the Rings (https://lotr.fandom.com/wiki/Main_Page)
- Game of Thrones (https://gameofthrones.fandom.com/wiki/Game_of_Thrones_Wiki).

These wikis are the home of knowledge for their topic. This is something you can become for your buzzword, and that should be the aim. Some of you may now be thinking, 'That's great, but how does it actually impact my bottom line?' That's a great question, and one pretty easily answered.

If you are able to create a reasonable quantity of high quality content that covers a broad spectrum of your given buzzword then, as mentioned in the previous chapter, you will begin to see gains in your search ranking (all other things being equal). The higher your website and content ranks, the more trustworthy it is perceived by Google, and the same applies for people too.

The deeper, the more detailed, the more accurate, and more to-the-point you can make your content, the more authoritative it will become. This authority will translate into sales because of trust. Hard-earned trust. Your work in building a database, a library of content around your common thread, shows that your knowledge isn't fleeting, nor is it vague or ill-thought-out.

This knowledge base will not only help you to sell to interested parties in the here and now, but also capture the thoughts and feelings of those who are purely researching the market, and are not yet ready to buy. These are the people who are researching the market, looking at what goods and services are on offer, at what price, and from whom. These people are at the awareness and information gathering stage of the buying journey. Exactly where your highly relevant content will be focused!

At this early stage your content is not only showcasing your knowledge, but placing you in a much stronger selling position than your competitors, who are purely trying to compete on price or after-sale service. You are effectively looking to give these prospects as many possible reasons to buy a good or service like yours in the first instance, but ultimately come back to you when they are ready to buy, because you have been the most helpful.

In the present, your potential customers are also looking for answers, potentially the same as in the earlier stage, and potentially to more specific questions. In addition, they will more than likely have a potential choice between your company and one or two others. At this time, they will have a number of internal considerations to ponder. This will include things like price, location, shipping costs, installation, support, and of course, are they a business I know will do a good job?

Specifically, on that last point, your content, and more importantly your dedication to be, as John Espirian puts it as 'relentlessly helpful' as possible will define you. This will help potential customers to trust you and buy from you. Remember the old – 'Like, Know, Trust' thing, well, it still works.

Becoming the wiki of your industry for your given buzz-word doesn't stop at attracting and converting new customers. It goes further. It helps you retain customers too. Sounds a little crazy, right? I can confirm though, that I am not crazy, I'm in fact deadpan serious.

Your consistently produced, highly relevant content will keep your customers coming back. This will create not one, but two, three, four, five or more touch points. With each touch point you become more memorable, and more valuable to the customer. And, as long as you keep providing the content they are craving, this becomes a bit of a self-fulfilling prophecy, because the more they interact with your content, the more in tune with your brand they are, the deeper your relationship goes, and the less likely they are to leave.

You have to keep at the front of your mind, that every time there is an interaction between you, your brand and your potential, or existing customers, you have a chance to deepen the relationship. I am also a firm believer that you must create your content a bit like how you would look to build a relationship with any individual you've met, or want to speak to, online or even at a physical business event.

There are few things worse than being at a business event and having the same starting conversation with 10, 20, 30 + other people. 'Hi my name is ....., what's yours? What do you do? How long have you been doing that?' You know – the same old questions over and over.

This is something you wouldn't want in a conversation, and also something that you wouldn't want when reading some content. You have to be a bit innovative and different in order to capture and hold people's attention. Even if they are existing clients, because it's not a given that they will stay customers.

Julia McCoy Case Study

When I was thinking about who I could bring on as an amazing case study for working on becoming a Wiki-pedia for their industry (content marketing); I didn't have to look very far. Julia McCoy, the CEO of Express Writers (https://expresswriters.com) is doing just this. The question now is... how?

Even though Julia now has a successful business and a growing reputation within the content marketing space, she wasn't always headed in this direction. In fact, it was only during college that she began to realise she wasn't doing what she loved. She knew that she wouldn't be happy.

Then came the lightbulb moment, that flash of reality. And, instead of carrying on like nothing could be done, she acted on it. This lightbulb moment was the realisation that she needed to make money doing something she loved. That was writing.

The next thing Julia did was amazing. She took the leap. She found websites like Upwork, elance and o-desk, started a profile, and began making money writing. Because she just did it, and took this leap, she found herself ahead of the curve, and managed to build a reputation before the competition became too fierce.

Over time Julia realised that marketers were crying out for content and quality writers. So, Julia dropped out of college, and in May 2011 began writing full-time. She then coded her own website, grew a group of quality writers, who above all had a love for writing... Express Writers was born.

Since then, the content marketing industry has grown exponentially. Today, there are so many agencies and freelancers. Far more than in 2011, and this trend will continue. In order to stand out Julia has built Express Writers to be about the story, not about the money.

Every writer on their books is vetted to ensure they actually have a love of writing.

In 2015, Julia pivoted slightly to focus on the content strategy side of things. She began asking the question: how can we really help our clients get a return from investing in content strategy?

This is where Julia started becoming a wiki of her industry. She started listening to her customers (not her competitors), processing their questions and working out the why. Julia and Express Writers then began to create helpful, valuable content that answered the queries and concerns of specialists in the industry.

For Julia, it's about being pro-active. There is no benchmark for being strategic. It takes a lot of work, over a long period of time.

As I write this case study, I can confidently say that Julia and Express Writers are now being seen by many as an authority within the content marketing space. It's taken time. But now, there is a podcast, a number of books, and a thriving business. That's taken years to get to, not weeks or months.

The hard part is constantly creating and maintaining this 'thought-leadership'. It takes time for original ideas to manifest themselves and for the whole company to buy-into. It's also an on-going process. Julia constantly works on her own self-growth. What I loved about speaking to Julia, was hearing her relentless drive for not letting her audience down.

Throughout Express Writers, there is a recognition of the importance of consistency. This consistency, Julia believes, is integral to the expert status she and her company are being labelled with, even if they wouldn't refer to themselves as experts. She also points out very clearly that to remain consistent, you have to avoid burn-out of ideas, thoughts and time. Delegation is essential for this. It helps Julia to spread the load, and helps the company to grow.

What I love about Julia is that she's been doing exactly what I set out in this book. The idea of building a personal brand, within a business brand, with a common thread running throughout. She doesn't see her personal brand as a separate brand to Express Writers, but an extension of it.

It's allowed her and her company to reach people they would never have before. It meant she and the company no longer had to outreach to people for new sales, but the sales came to them.

Instead of wasting time reading hundreds of websites, and trying to create loads of different content types, Julia reads from just 5 publishers now, and focuses on formats that are going to do well, or that either herself or her business can do better/differently. The knowledge Julia gains is ploughed back into the business.

If Julia wasn't building her personal brand as well as building the business, neither would be as successful. I'm so excited to see what's still to come from Julia and Express Writers!

The story of Julia and Express Writers is not unique to the world. It's an amazing example of how to build a company around a common thread, and become known as experts within the industry. Julia not only talks-the-talk, but walks-the-walk. The effort and detail she puts into her personal brand and business brand is incredible, and it's an honour to see both develop.

Turning this back on you. How can you help your customers? How can you be the font of knowledge for your buzzword? And, what can you create that will help establish a clear link between you, your business and your buzzword? Remember, to put yourself in your audience's shoes, it's not about you, it's about them. Think all the way back to chapter twelve of this book. You need to answer questions in a way that your audience can consume and understand. If you do that, you will begin to build a bank of useful content and start to be seen as a wiki for your industry.

TASK: LIST 10-20 QUESTIONS YOUR AUDIENCE MAY ASK AROUND YOUR CHOSEN BUZZWORD. THINK ABOUT QUESTIONS THAT HELP IMPROVE YOUR AUDIENCES UNDERSTANDING AND ADD CONTEXT TO YOUR BUZZWORD.

Think about positioning yourself as the trusted voice in your industry by providing helpful content which helps people make good buying decisions.

- John Espirian, Espirian

The Marketing Buzzword Podcast

TWENTY-TWO
FINDING THE RIGHT BUZZWORD & INTEGRATING IT

"One of the best paradoxes of leadership is a leader's need to be both stubborn and open-minded. A leader must insist on sticking to the vision and stay on course to the destination. But he must be open-minded during the process."

- Simon Sinek

I n this final chapter I want to challenge you to decide exactly what it is you stand for. What term defines you and your business? How will people know you? What are you currently, or are you going to become an expert in?

This is always a difficult process, and I've found a good brainstorming session (or do we have to call them a thought shower or ideation session now?) with your peers, employees and others in the industry can help to narrow this down.

It's also important to look back at the chapter earlier in the book on coining your own term, or leveraging the opportunities presented by a term that's already in existence. This is because whichever route you choose to go down, you will have a slightly different set of advantages and drawbacks.

In order to draw out which route is right for you and the business, these brainstorming sessions will have to look at a number of considerations such as:

How long will the buzzword likely last? Is it fleeting?

Do we have a term we use inside the business a lot?

Is this something our employees can buy into?

Does a market already exist?

From a business's perspective there are a lot more moving parts and factors which can affect the chosen buzzword and direction, compared to choosing one for a personal brand. These are important to address though:

How long will the buzzword last?

It's pretty much impossible to know exactly, but there are some tell-tale signs. When a buzzword gets massive traction early on but there isn't a clear reason why it exists, or the purpose it is going to have, that's a warning sign. Or, if it's tied into and relies on something else not changing, in a quickly changing world.

Something that Jessika Phillips noted in her case study was that the reason she feels so confident in 'relationship marketing' as a buzzword that will stand the test of time is that it's a way of thinking, a philosophy. It's not tied to a time, a place or a technology. It is instead a way of being.

If your buzzword isn't tied to technological advancements or certain platforms, then it will stand a better chance of lasting longer. Do remember though, that longer isn't always better, because the shorter-lived buzzwords can help you to grow an audience quicker.

There's no exact science, but the odds are definitely better.

Do we have a term we use within the business a lot?

Having a term which is yours, and something unique which you can add to people's vocabulary. If you have a unique way to describe a certain set of circumstances, activities or a process, can you use that as your buzzword? Taking Hubspot as an example again with 'inbound marketing', this described a marketing process and set of activities to draw leads into the business instead of traditional outbound marketing.

If you don't have an existing term, can you create one that describes a specific set of activities like 'conversational commerce' or 'Social Intelligence'? Or, like Yext did with the term 'Digital Knowledge Management'?

Is this something our employees can buy into?

As a business you have your employees to think about, and they could be an integral piece of your buzzword jigsaw. You need to make sure that they can buy into and are able to work to the company's common thread.

Without your employees' buy-in, you are likely to struggle to build your presence related to the buzzword with true conviction, and at a reasonable pace. You cannot forget your employees when you are trying to build your business's authority.

Does a market already exist?

If you are going to align your business with an already existing buzzword, you will need to do lots of research into how current competitors shape-up, look at potential gaps in the market and find a way to stand out.

Just because a market is crowded, it doesn't mean the buzzword you are trying to get known for is wrong. You can localise, specialise or generalise. Take for instance the terms 'social media marketing' and 'content marketing'. There are thousands upon thousands of businesses for all different industries and locations, but the common thread is that all are based around content marketing.

Brands like Social Media Examiner (https://www. socialmediaexaminer.com) didn't enter into the world of social media from the outset. They came in slightly later, but they dominated their sphere by being different and focussing on the needs of their audience and by giving consistent value.

The above are just a sample of the types of questions you need to be asking of yourselves and other stakeholders within the business. It isn't always an easy thing to get agreement, but being laser-focused on becoming the go-to company in the market for your given buzzword will help you to become the authority your industry needs.

Just like with personal branding; just because you have built / are building / have just started to build a brand around a buzzword, it doesn't mean that you are tied to it indefinitely. As industries and technologies change, you can (and should) adapt to survive.

The key to this though is communication and not chopping and changing regularly. As a business it's going to be more challenging to shift position, and harder still as your business and number of employees grows.

Socialbakers Case Study

Socialbakers is a company that I have so much time for. They have a fantastic reputation, and the reason that I wanted to include them as a case study is because I see them as an organisation that embodies what I am suggesting in this book.

They have also had to change over time, to stay relevant and to still be seen as a leading company in the social media and marketing space. That is why they were perfect for this book.

Originally Socialbakers was highly focused on the social media marketing space with regards to Facebook marketing. They actually started off as a social media agency called Candytech. However, as time has progressed, they have had to evolve, firstly becoming Socialbakers and now to focus more on becoming a social media management platform, based on artificial intelligence technologies.

Not only have Socialbakers had to pivot slightly in terms of focus, they have also had to ensure that all members of their global, growing workforce are on the same wavelength. They have to make sure that no matter where in the world their employees are located, they all understand and buy into what Socialbakers is all about, and what the company stands for.

With all that in mind, I spoke to Moses Velasco, who at the time was Chief of Strategy for Socialbakers to find out what their common thread was, and how they maintained it throughout the business.

His response was simple: Data and Social Media Intelligence is the core thread. Even though Social Media was the vehicle to help drive it forward. Data and intel-ligence is at the core of Socialbakers.

I wasn't just interested in what their thread was, I was also intrigued as to how they could maintain this thread throughout the business, no matter where in the world their people or offices are located. Moses said that they do this by asking three key questions of themselves.

1. What are we passionate about? – Helping customers to make the most out of their data.
2. What are we best at? – Analytics, data and combining the two to make smart recommendations.
3. Where can we make money? – Providing tools and services to help businesses get more value out of their social media marketing.

These questions, together, help to focus what Social-bakers does as a business. They are building out from data. Coming up with new ideas, new algorithms, and utilising the latest technologies.

At first, they channelled that primarily through social media marketing and now also through influencer marketing and audience segmentation. No matter which channel they are operating in, the thread remains the same.

Socialbakers truly believes that providing customers with social media intelligence is the future, and by investing in this growth area, they will see huge gains in the years to come.

It's not enough for Socialbakers to sell this thread internally, they have to sell the concept and ideas to potential customers. Separately that can be a challenge in itself, but together it's even more so. So how is it possible?

Their response; to create simplicity. They want to ask and answer the fundamental questions surrounding the industry, for both their employees and their customers. Questions like 'what do marketers do every day?' and 'how can we simplify the lives of marketers?' They then seek to answer the who, what, when, where, why and how questions which follow.

As a company though, they don't deal in guesswork or putting out surveys. They are using data and AI to provide marketers with the best possible recommendations for their campaigns right now. It's not just the reporting of the data either, it's also the analysis to help the marketers to make better decisions about their campaigns and where to invest.

I love this because it's not only completely in-line with their common thread, but it's also practicing what they preach.

I'm also a big admirer of the fact that they aren't a business that's getting stuck with the old mantra of 'that's always worked for us'. They are constantly looking to evolve based upon their customers' needs and wants. If the customers start voting with their feet (or more aptly, clicks) then the business may need to refocus its efforts.

There is still so much to come from Socialbakers in the coming years, and I cannot wait to see what new ideas and tools they come up with going forward!

Make sure you take a look at the Socialbakers website and technology. It's really good: https://www.socialbakers.com

I'm a big fan of Socialbakers as a brand. They found a niche, built a business within it, and are now pivoting and expanding their horizons in order to keep growing and stay at the forefront of a quickly changing industry.

This is no mean feat, especially with employees all over the world. But as this case study demonstrates, it is entirely possible and it is within your reach. You just have to embrace it.

Years ago the definition of a brand is what the business told you it was. But, with social media the customer owns the brand, and it is what they say it is. As a company, you can try to influence those perceptions, but you can't tell them what they think it is.

- Dennis Owen, Hong Kong Airlines

The Marketing Buzzword Podcast

CONCLUSION

Throughout the entirety of this book, I have aimed to broaden horizons: the horizons of you, your peers and the industry at large. I want us, as marketers and business people, to aspire to something more than simply using buzzwords as a means to sound clever, or to bamboozle your peers.

We must remember that it's our job, as industry professionals, to help teach people what buzzwords mean, give them context and uphold standards. We must hold ourselves to a higher standard than just blindly using words and phrases. It's not about using more buzzwords; it's about being smarter with the buzzwords we do use.

Whether you work for yourself and are talking to clients or prospects on a daily basis, or lead your own marketing team, you have to ensure that everyone is using the same standardised language and that you not only know what the words are but have the context in which to action it.

When you use a buzzword; whether it's your own, or one that already exists, you have to simplify it all. You cannot assume that everyone else has the knowledge you do. You have to be a teacher, you have to make sure that both you and your audience understand the fundamentals before you can go deeper. You owe that to yourself and your audience.

Remember: it's not about you, it's never about you. It's about adding value. That's how you become known in this crowded world. It's not about who has the most fans, or who has the most positive mentions. It's about giving people the knowledge and ideas to forge their own path. It doesn't matter if that's two people or two hundred, as long as you can run your business with that many people.

There is room for everyone. Don't think that by teaching others how to do what you do, you are going to lose out on customers to them. You may lose some customers, sure, it would be silly to say that was inconceivable. However, what you will do is gain more customers because of your reputation for helping.

Have you ever heard of a teacher that taught too well, that they never got any more work because everyone had the knowledge? No. Have you ever heard of an expert that stopped being an expert because everyone else was? No. There may be a range of other reasons why they may not be an expert any more, but I can guarantee it is not because they ran out of people to teach.

When you find your word, you have to put your all into it. It's not good enough just to know it. You have to add your personality, and you have to be consistent. And, most importantly you have to make sure that you provide context so that others can buy into what you're selling (your buzzword). Can you answer the question 'what's in it for them?'

Can you give your audience the knowledge they seek, in a

way that they understand, and is enjoyable for them to consume? All the while, remembering to keep it simple...

It sounds a lot, right? Well, it is and it isn't.

You can make things easier on yourself. You can do this by finding places and spaces that suit you, that fit your style, and give you the ability to clearly communicate. It's not about being in all places, trying to reach as many people as possible. It's about doing a small number of things very well. If you want, you can go all-in on one channel and aim for mastery of the single area. But this is not for everyone and could lessen your opportunities in the future. The choice is yours. The rewards are yours.

Whether you are an individual aligning yourself to a buzz-word, or a business with a number of employees trying to find a common thread, both can benefit. It is not one at the expense of the other. It is mutual.

Personal branding is entwined with what is referred to as traditional business branding. In a digital age, the lines between both aren't just close, they are wrapped up in each other.

The personal brands that exist within a business are an extension of the businesses brand, and vice versa. The actions of one represent the other, and what they stand for also reflects both. This includes the buzzwords and terminology they are associated with.

People in the 21st century want to be aligned with something. A cause, or a business that they believe in. It's no longer the case of the biggest brands that pay the biggest salaries win every time, or the brands with the cheapest prices. Both customers and potential employees are far fickler, and so much more sceptical than at any time previous.

That commonality can be a buzzword. A word or phrase

everyone buys into and understands. It doesn't have to be something elaborate or extreme. It can be simple. Simple is effective.

Now, I want you to take this, all of this book and make it your reality. Take the world as it is, and make it better. Make it simpler, and make it clearer. And, most importantly, don't use words and phrases for the sake of it, or to sound clever. It doesn't work!

REFERENCES

1. What exactly is a buzzword, and is it the same as jargon?

1. https://www.inc.com/james-sudakow/the-89-worst-business-buzzwords-of-all-time.html
2. https://www.bbc.co.uk/news/technology-42657621

4. The psychology of buzzwords

1. https://www.imdb.com/title/tto114781/
2. https://journals.sagepub.com/doi/abs/10.2190/J8JJ-4YD0-4R00-G5N0
3. https://www.urbandictionary.com/

II. Buzzwords for Personal Branding

1. https://personalbrand.com/definition/

9. Should I coin my own, or use a buzzword that already exists?

1. https://businessesgrow.com/2014/01/06/content-shock/
2. https://www.bryankramer.com/there-is-no-more-b2b-or-b2c-its-human-to-human-h2h/
3. https://dictionary.cambridge.org/dictionary/english/a-snowball-effect
4. https://en.wikipedia.org/wiki/Thought_leader
5. Winning at Social Customer Care

11. A personal brand has personality

1. https://en.wikipedia.org/wiki/Churchill_Insurance

15. How not to build a personal brand around a buzzword

1. My Book
2. https://startwithwhy.com
3. https://www.bbc.co.uk/news/health-38896790

III. Buzzwords for Business

1. https://www.ons.gov.uk/employmentandlabourmarket/peopleinwork/employmentandemployeetypes/bulletins/uklabourmarket/july2018

18. Using a buzzword as a common thread

1. https://idioms.thefreedictionary.com/common+thread
2. http://www.businessdictionary.com/definition/strategic-alignment.html

19. Using personal brands within existing business brands

1. https://www.investopedia.com/terms/i/intrapreneurship.asp

INDEX

ACKNOWLEDGMENTS

There are a number of people I would like to thank in particular for their help guidance and contributions which have made this book possible.

Chris and Sarah, my parents, without your dedication, love and support I don't think this would have been possible. You've been there when I needed you, and you left me to it when I was "in the zone". I could not ask for a better set of parents.

To **everyone at Talkative**. Thank you for putting up with all my rants about marketing buzzwords and supporting me with the growth of my Marketing Buzzword Podcast. Without your encouragement and understanding, the podcast would not be what it is today.

Meg, my beautiful girlfriend. Thank you for putting up with me during my long nights and early mornings. Through all of my ups and downs you have been there to help me. You are my rock.

To my **friends and family**. I can't thank you enough for your understanding my lack of communication and for helping to motivate me to create this book.

Mark Masters, you have been an amazing source of ideas, inspiration and guidance. Your encouragement and support has been has been immeasurable.

Chris Strub, I cannot thank you enough, for your words of encouragement, guidance and wisdom. You have helped keep me on track, and kept me believing. This book wouldn't be what it is without you.

To **Dan Gingiss, Bryan Kramer, John Espirian, Julia McCoy, Jessika Phillips, Sonja Jefferson, Mark Masters, Kelly Noble Mirabella, Yext** and **Socialbakers** Thank you so much for being amazing case studies. You all epitomise what I want this book to be about. You've all been so grateful in giving up for time, insights and knowledge. Without your case studies, this book would not have the impact I want it to.

I'd also like to thank all of my podcast guests for helping me with my project to debunk and demystify marketing buzzwords. Without you, the podcast would not exist, without the podcast, this book wouldn't exist, so i'd like to thank the following guests who have been on the podcast before and during the creation of this book:

- Dan Gingiss (Persado) - Social Customer Service
- Nicky Kriel (Nicky Kriel) - Social Selling
- Jessika Phillips (NOW Marketing Group) - Relationship Marketing
- Mark Masters (The ID Group and You Are The Media) - Great Content

- Ash Phillips (YENA) - Millennial Marketing
- Chris Marr (Content Marketing Academy) - Community
- Andrew and Pete (Atomic) - Engaging Content
- Tracey Smolinski (Introbiz) - Networking
- Kerry L Watt (Rising Tide Media) - Authority Marketing
- Barry Schwartz (Rusty Brick & SEO Roundtable) - Search Engine Optimisation
- Bryan Kramer (Pure Matter) - Humanisation
- Elizabeth Clark (Dream Agility) - Machine Learning
- Joey Coleman (Joey Coleman) - Customer Experience
- Brian Fanzo (iSocialFanz) - Personal Branding
- Duane Forrester & Dave Ciancio (Yext) - Digital Knowledge Management
- Paul Ince (Like Mind Media) - Event Marketing
- Chris Strub (I am Here LLC) - Live Streaming
- John Espirian (Espirian Technical Copywriting) - Copywriting
- Ashley Dudarenok (ChoZan & Alarice) - Entrepreneur
- Angus Nelson (Life of Dad) - Influencer Marketing
- Madalyn Sklar (Madalyn Sklar) - Conversational Marketing
- Moses Velasco (Socialbakers) - Buzzwords
- Tim Addison (SEM Rush) - Paid Search
- Mordecai Holtz (Blue Thread Marketing) - User Generated Content
- Andrew Davis (Brandscaping) - Video Marketing
- Katie Clift (Katie Clift PR) - PR

- Adam Buchanan (Adam Buchanan Consulting) - Marketing Trust
- Ryan Pena (Be The Match) - Social Good
- Mark Asquith (Excellence Expected) - Podcasting
- Chris Roberts (Cybata) - GDPR
- Bella Vasta (Jump Consulting) - Facebook Groups
- Dennis Owen (Hong Kong Airways) - Branding
- Desiree Martinez (All-in-One Social Media) - Social Contesting
- Tim Lewis (Stoneham Press) - Self Publishing
- Craig Barnett (Culturvate) - Corporate Culture
- Rob Watson (Freewheeling) - PPC & Pay-to-Play
- Shep Hyken (Hyken) - Convenience
- Michael Berean (Grace Innovation) - Gamification
- Chrstine Gritmon (Christine Gritmon inc) - Meaningful Interactions
- Kerry Harrison & Richard Norton (Tiny Giant) - Creative AI
- Ben Ellis (Brandwatch) - Social Intelligence
- Kelly Noble Mirabella (Stellar Media) - Chatbots
- Jen Cole (DepICT Media) - Tribe
- Julia McCoy (Express Writers) - Snackable Content
- Rob Balasabas (Thinkific) - Online Courses
- Peter Sumpton (Marketing Study Lab) - Marketing Qualifications
- Nicole Osborne (Lollipop Social) - Behind-the-Scenes Content
- Dr Ai Addison-Zhang (Classroom Without Walls) - Human Connections
- Roger Edwards (Roger Edwards Marketing) - Buzzwords Vs Jargon

- Jon Burkhart (TBC Global) - Brand Storytelling
- Cathy Wassell (Socially Contented) - Lead Generation

ABOUT THE AUTHOR

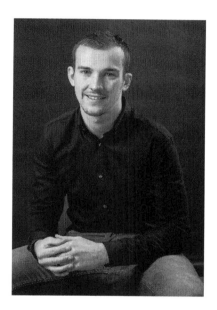

Ben M Roberts is the founder and host of The Marketing Buzzword Podcast, Head of Marketing at Talkative, a SaaS Technology Start-Up and an international conference speaker. In 2018 he was also named Wales' No1 businessman under 35.

Ben's podcast boasts thousands of unique listeners around the world, and he has interviewed some of the biggest names in marketing, to help break down common marketing buzzwords to the sum of their parts. In addition to the podcast, Ben also speaks about marketing buzzwords and personal branding at conferences in the UK and beyond. He also contributes to notable online business & marketing publications, with a growing portfolio of media features and mentions from across the UK and around the world.

During the day, Ben can be found as Head of Marketing at a rapidly expanding Startup Technology company called Talkative. At Talkative, Ben has built the marketing department from scratch. This includes everything from putting together the strategy, ensuring the website was best placed to rank highly in search engines, establishing a reporting suite and hiring new team members, to physically writing content and negotiating deals with industry experts.

Prior to his role at Talkative, Ben was Head of Marketing at a Top 100 UK Insurance Broker (Moorhouse Group), and before that Marketing Strategist at a large, specialist eCommerce website (Heinnie.com). This has helped to give Ben a broad understanding of differences in digital marketing across various industries both B2B and B2C.He has made an incredible number of mistakes and had even more success on route to today. All of those experiences he now wants to use to help other people develop their businesses and careers.

Book Ben as a speaker

If you like what you've read in this book, you can hire Ben to come and speak at your event or conference, or you get him to put on a workshop to help you and your business apply to principles set out throughout the entirety of the book.

Please send Ben an email to ben@ben-m-roberts.com for more information or to enquire about getting him to your event.

twitter.com/Roberts_Ben_M

37607986R00148

Printed in Poland
by Amazon Fulfillment
Poland Sp. z o.o., Wrocław